I0762514

THE SEASONAL PANTRY

by Benoît Castel

75
HOMEMADE RECIPES
TO WASTE LESS
AND ENJOY MORE

Photography by Guillaume Czerw

tra.publishing

Introduction

Down to Earth

For several years now, I've made the respect of raw ingredients and waste reduction central to everything I do in my bakeries and pastry shops. It's not revolutionary. It's simply a return to common sense. So when the idea of starting a vegetable garden in Brittany took root two years ago, it only deepened my commitment. The garden has helped me understand seasonality even better, something that's always shaped my work as a pastry chef. My team and I enjoy picking out the seed varieties we'll grow. I look forward to seeing each crop appear, and there's nothing like topping off a dessert with fruit harvested at peak ripeness. I say "topping," but the smashed, ripe berries, hidden in the whipped cream inside a tart shell finished with a crumble, are actually the centerpiece.

A Whole Lot of Sauce

A garden sometimes means a glut of fruit and vegetables—and that's something to celebrate. It's the perfect chance to make delicious preserves and flavorful jams. When you cook your overflowing stock of oranges with sugar to make marmalade, it's not just a penchant for flavor: it's a survival instinct for the fruit to live on through the seasons. Whether it's jars of green beans or wine-poached pears, tomato sauce, or pickles, the garden's flavors can be enjoyed all year round.

And to truly respect the produce, we waste nothing. Got vegetable peels? Make stock. Got overripe fruit? Boil it with sugar and tea, and you'll have a wonderful iced tea.

Back to the Future

The other great thing about treating ingredients with reverence is being able to cook today so you can eat well tomorrow, even when time is short. Around the same time I planted the garden, I opened a grocery shop in Paris's Ménilmontant neighborhood. I wanted to offer ready-to-use artisan-made bases: things like puff pastry, meringues for pavlovas, and prebaked sweet and savory tart shells. I also wanted to sell sauces, pralinés, and plant-based milks—all things you'll be happy to find stocked in your pantry and refrigerator. That's what I've aimed to share in this book: how to prep ingredients and bases that keep well so you can turn them into meals or desserts later. That's the spirit of my pantry: cooking high-quality ingredients for future use without wasting a crumb.

A Note for All Recipes

Unless critical to the final result, I've intentionally left the amounts of salt, pepper, and spices up to your discretion. Unless specified otherwise, eggs are large, butter is unsalted, flour is all-purpose, sugar is granulated, and salt is kosher. In addition, purchasing untreated or organic citrus is expensive, but it's well worth it when recipes call for zest. If that's not an option, wash your citrus, as well as all of your fruits and vegetables, well before using.

Contents

1

SWEET AND SAVORY DOUGHS

These handmade doughs can be prepped in advance and assembled on demand. That means they're ready to cook or bake for a delicious meal whenever the time comes. They are also versatile enough to take creative liberties—why not try savory cream puffs or a sweet vol-au-vent?

Savory Tart Dough

This dough can be used for any savory quiche (page 20) or tart. Make sure to check the dough measurements for each recipe because this base recipe makes more than is usually called for.

MAKES ABOUT 1 LB (450 G)
PREP TIME: 15 MINUTES
BAKE TIME: 30 MINUTES

2 CUPS (250 G) FLOUR
9 TBSP BUTTER, SOFTENED (PLUS EXTRA FOR GREASING)
1 TSP SALT
6 TBSP COLD WATER
½ TBSP WHITE VINEGAR

Preheat the oven to 325°F (160°C).

In a large bowl, combine the flour and butter and rub them between your fingers until the mixture feels sandy. This coats the gluten with fat and makes the dough crumbly.

In a small bowl, dissolve the salt in the water. Add both the salted water and vinegar to the flour mixture. On a clean surface, knead the dough with the palm of your hand until it is smooth and slightly elastic, 3 to 5 minutes.

To blind bake, roll out the dough to about ⅛ inch (3 mm) thick. Grease an 8-inch (20-cm) tart pan and line it with enough dough to cover and press it down with your fingers. Reserve the remaining dough for another use. Cut a 9.5-inch (24-cm) circle of parchment paper and place it over the dough. Fill with pie weights or dried beans and blind bake the crust for 30 minutes.

Remove from the oven and cool to room temperature, wrap in plastic, and freeze for later. There's no need to defrost frozen crusts before use. Just remove from the freezer, fill, and bake per recipe instructions.

Garden Vegetable Quiches

Several combinations follow, but feel free to use whichever veggies you have on hand.

SERVES 6
PREP TIME: 20 MINUTES
BAKE TIME: 1 HOUR 30 MINUTES

SAVORY TART DOUGH (PAGE 17) OR A PREBAKED 8-INCH (20-CM) TART SHELL
BUTTER, FOR GREASING

QUICHE CUSTARD BASE

⅔ CUP (150 G) CRÈME FRAÎCHE
⅔ CUP (160 ML) HEAVY CREAM
6 EGGS
FRESHLY GRATED NUTMEG
SALT AND PEPPER

SWEET PEA FILLING

SALT
2 CUPS (300 G) FRESH PEAS
2 SPRIGS FRESH MINT, LEAVES FINELY CHOPPED

GREEN BEAN FILLING

SALT
2 CUPS (300 G) GREEN BEANS, TRIMMED
1 PACKED CUP (30 G) BEET GREENS
1 TSP BUTTER

ZUCCHINI-GOAT CHEESE FILLING

1 GREEN ZUCCHINI
1 YELLOW ZUCCHINI
1 GREEN BELL PEPPER
7 OZ (200 G) FRESH GOAT CHEESE

LESCURE
CRÈME
ENTIÈRE
35

Garden Vegetable Quiches

Preheat the oven to 325°F (160°C) if blind baking the tart dough. Preheat to 340°F (170°C) if you have a prebaked tart shell.

To make the quiche custard base, in a mixing bowl, whisk together the crème fraîche and heavy cream. Add the eggs and a pinch each of freshly grated nutmeg, salt, and pepper. Mix until the eggs are thoroughly incorporated.

If the savory tart dough has not been prebaked, butter an 8-inch (20-cm) tart pan. Roll out the dough to about ⅛ inch (3 mm) thick. Gently lift the dough like a tablecloth to relax it, then place it in the prepared tart pan (reserve any leftover dough for another use). Prick the dough on the base with a fork. Place parchment paper over the dough and fill with pie weights or dried beans. Bake for 30 minutes—the base should remain slightly underdone to protect it during the final bake. Remove from the oven, carefully remove the pie weights, and cool.

In the meantime, make the filling of your choice.

Sweet Pea Filling

To make the sweet pea filling, bring a large pot of salted water to a boil. Blanch the peas for 5 minutes, then shock them in ice water to preserve their color. Combine the peas with the mint.

Green Bean Filling

To make the green bean filling, bring a large pot of salted water to a boil. Blanch the green beans for 5 minutes, then plunge into ice water. In a skillet, wilt the beet greens in the butter. Combine the green beans and wilted beet greens.

Zucchini-Goat Cheese Filling

To make the zucchini-goat cheese filling, using a mandoline, slice the zucchini and bell pepper into ribbons and set aside. Crumble the goat cheese over the base of the prebaked crust and top with the zucchini and bell pepper ribbons.

Pour the chosen filling into the prepared tart shell. Fill to the top with the custard base and bake at 340°F (170°C) for 1 hour or until the crust is golden brown and the center of the quiche barely jiggles. Insert a knife about an inch from the edge and, if it comes out clean, it's ready. Remove quiche from the oven and let cool completely. Run a knife around the tart ring to release the crust.

Inverted Puff Pastry Dough

This staple dough is incredibly flaky and light. Make a batch of it now and use it later in dishes such as Alsatian Flatbread (page 28), Roasted Apricot Pizza (page 31), and Strawberry & Lemon Vol-au-Vent (page 32).

MAKES ABOUT 2 LBS (900 G)
PREP TIME: 40 MINUTES
CHILL TIME: 6 HOURS

BUTTER BLOCK

1 CUP (120 G) FLOUR
1 ⅓ CUPS (320 G) COLD BUTTER

DOUGH BASE

2 TSP SALT
½ CUP (120 ML) COLD WATER
6 TBSP BUTTER, MELTED
2 ¼ CUPS (280 G) FLOUR
2 PINCHES SUGAR

To make the butter block, mix the flour and butter in the bowl of a stand mixer fitted with the paddle attachment until just combined—the texture should be smooth and homogeneous.

Between two sheets of parchment paper, roll the butter into a neat rectangle about ½ inch (1 cm) thick. Chill in the refrigerator until firm, at least 30 minutes.

To make the dough base, in a small bowl, dissolve the salt into the cold water.

In the bowl of a stand mixer fitted with a dough hook, add the melted butter, salted water, flour, and sugar.

Mix on low speed for 8 minutes, then on medium for 3 minutes until the dough is smooth and cohesive.

Roll the dough between two sheets of parchment paper into a rectangle half the size of the butter block. Chill for at least 1 hour.

Remove both the butter block and the dough base from the refrigerator. On a clean surface, place the dough on top of the butter block and roll both the butter and dough in one direction to form a long, even rectangle.

Give the dough and butter a single fold (letter fold), wrap in parchment paper or plastic wrap, and chill for 2 hours.

Roll out the combined dough and give it two double folds (book folds), then chill for another 2 hours.

Roll out the dough one last time, perform a final single fold, then roll the dough out to about ¹⁄₁₂ inch (2 mm) thick. Prick the surface all over with a fork and let it rest in the fridge for 1 hour.

At this point, follow the recipe that calls for puff pastry or freeze your dough by wrapping it in plastic; it will keep for 1 month. Simply defrost in the refrigerator the night before you plan to use it.

Alsatian Flatbread

SERVES 6
PREP TIME: 10 MINUTES
BAKE TIME: 30 MINUTES

10½ OZ (300 G) INVERTED PUFF PASTRY DOUGH (PAGE 24)
⅔ CUP (150 G) CRÈME FRAÎCHE
⅔ CUP (150 G) NONFAT PLAIN GREEK YOGURT OR FROMAGE BLANC
FRESHLY GRATED NUTMEG
SALT AND PEPPER
10 SLICES COOKED BACON, CUT INTO ¾-INCH (2-CM) PIECES
2 SPRIGS FRESH THYME, LEAVES ONLY

Preheat the oven to 400°F (200°C).

On a lightly floured surface, roll out the puff pastry dough into a disk about ⅛ inch (3 mm) thick.

In a small bowl, mix the crème fraîche and yogurt together. Season with the nutmeg, salt, and pepper.

Spread the mixture evenly over the raw puff pastry, right up to the edges. Distribute the bacon and thyme leaves over the top.

Bake for 30 minutes or until the crust is golden brown and the sauce is bubbly. Serve immediately.

Roasted Apricot Pizza

SERVES 6
PREP TIME: 10 MINUTES
COOK TIME: 15 MINUTES

1½ TBSP BUTTER
1 HEAPING TBSP HONEY
15 APRICOTS, HALVED
5 OZ (150 G) APRICOT-ROSEMARY JAM (PAGE 116)
INVERTED PUFF PASTRY DOUGH (PAGE 24) OR ONE 9-INCH (22-CM) PIZZA DOUGH BASE
1 SPRIG ROSEMARY, LEAVES ONLY

Preheat the oven to 400°F (200°C).

In a skillet, melt the butter with the honey over medium heat. Add the apricots and caramelize both sides, about 3 minutes.

If using puff pastry: On a lightly floured surface, roll out the puff pastry dough into a disk about ⅛ inch (3 mm) thick.

Spread the jam over the puff pastry or pizza base, arrange the apricots in a spiral pattern, and finish with the rosemary leaves.

Bake for 10 minutes and serve warm.

Strawberry & Lemon Vol-au-Vent

Think of a vol-au-vent as a small pastry frame that can be filled with sweet or savory treats—in this case lemon-olive oil cream and strawberries. While this dish is impressive, it's also surprisingly easy to make. For best results, serve immediately to preserve the crispness of the pastry.

MAKES 10
PREP TIME: 1 HOUR
COOK TIME: 50 MINUTES
CHILL TIME: 2 HOURS

1 LB (450 G) INVERTED PUFF PASTRY DOUGH (PAGE 24)
2 EGGS AND 1 YOLK
½ CUP (105 G) SUGAR
1 TBSP CORNSTARCH
⅓ CUP (80 ML) LEMON JUICE
½ CUP (120 ML) OLIVE OIL
2 PINTS STRAWBERRIES, HULLED AND HALVED

Line a baking sheet with parchment paper.

Roll out the Inverted Puff Pastry Dough to about 1⁄16 inch (1 ½ mm) thick. Prick with a fork.

Using a 3-inch (8-cm) square cutter, cut out 20 pieces of pastry. Place 10 squares on the prepared baking sheet.

Cut the centers out of the remaining squares with a 2 ½-inch (6-cm) square cutter to form frames.

Brush the edges of the whole squares with water and top each with a frame. Score the edges with the tip of a knife to seal. Refrigerate for 1 hour.

Preheat the oven to 400°F (200°C).

Bake for 10 minutes, then reduce the oven temperature to 320°F (160°C) and continue baking for 40 minutes.

To make the lemon cream, in a medium saucepan, whisk together the eggs, egg yolk, sugar, and cornstarch until light and smooth. Add the lemon juice and cook over medium heat, stirring constantly, until the mixture boils. Remove from the heat and allow to cool to about 120°F (50°C). Add the olive oil and blend with an immersion blender until smooth and emulsified.

Spread in a thin layer in a shallow dish, cover with plastic wrap pressed to the surface, and chill for 1 hour.

To assemble, cut the top off each vol-au-vent with a serrated knife.

Pipe about 3 tbsp of lemon cream into each shell, dress with the strawberries, and then top with the remaining top of the vol-au-vent.

Cocoa Sweet Pastry Dough

MAKES ABOUT 1 LB 4 OZ (570 G)
PREP TIME: 15 MINUTES
CHILL TIME: 2 HOURS

9 TBSP BUTTER, AT ROOM TEMPERATURE
⅔ CUP (128 G) SUGAR
1 ¾ CUPS (235 G) FLOUR, PLUS MORE FOR THE WORK SURFACE
2 TBSP UNSWEETENED COCOA POWDER
2 TSP BAKING POWDER
1 EGG
1 EGG YOLK
1 TSP VANILLA EXTRACT

Preheat the oven to 325°F (160°C).

In the bowl of a stand mixer fitted with the paddle attachment, cream together the butter and sugar until light and fluffy, about 3 minutes. Add the flour, cocoa powder, and baking powder, and mix until the dough takes on a crumbly, sandy texture. Incorporate the egg, egg yolk, and vanilla extract. Mix until just combined and a dough forms.

Cover the bowl with plastic wrap, and refrigerate for at least 2 hours.

Lightly flour your work surface. Roll out the dough gradually with a rolling pin, making sure it doesn't stick. Roll to about ⅛ inch (3 mm) thick and prick all over with a fork.

Cut the dough to fit the baking mold of your choice or follow the steps for Cocoa Florentines (page 150).

Choux Pastry Dough

This versatile pastry dough is the jumping-off point for recipes such as Choux-Style Buns with Parmesan Craquelin (page 37), Red Berry Profiteroles (page 41), or Vanilla & Chocolate Profiteroles (page 42).

MAKES 1 ½ LBS (675 G)
PREP TIME: 15 MINUTES

1 CUP (240 ML) WHOLE MILK
¾ TSP FINE SALT
¾ TSP SUGAR
7 TBSP BUTTER
1 CUP (130 G) FLOUR
4 EGGS

Preheat the oven to 340°F (170°C).

In a large saucepan, heat the milk, salt, sugar, and butter. Once it comes to a boil, remove from the heat and add the flour all at once. Stir vigorously until well combined.

Return the saucepan to the heat and cook, stirring continuously, until the dough forms a smooth, cohesive ball that no longer sticks to the pan.

Transfer to the bowl of a stand mixer fitted with the paddle attachment. Mix on low speed for 5 minutes to cool the dough slightly.

Add the eggs gradually, mixing well between each, until the dough reaches the "bird's beak" stage—meaning it should be smooth and fall from the spatula in a soft V shape.

Transfer the choux to a piping bag and either use immediately in recipes such as Choux-Style Buns with Parmesan Craquelin, Red Berry Profiteroles, or Vanilla & Chocolate Profiteroles or freeze. You can freeze the choux directly in the piping bag, just thaw it in the refrigerator the night before use.

Choux-Style Buns with Parmesan Craquelin

MAKES 8
PREP TIME: 30 MINUTES
CHILL TIME: 1 HOUR 15 MINUTES
COOK TIME: 30 MINUTES

PARMESAN CREAM

5 TBSP BUTTER
5 TBSP FLOUR
2 CUPS (480 ML) HEAVY CREAM
1 CUP (100 G) GRATED PARMESAN CHEESE
FRESHLY GRATED NUTMEG
SALT AND PEPPER

PARMESAN CRAQUELIN

5 ½ TBSP BUTTER, SOFTENED
5 ½ TBSP FLOUR
1 CUP (100 G) GRATED PARMESAN CHEESE

BUNS

1 LB 6 OZ (640 G) CHOUX PASTRY DOUGH (PAGE 35)
8 THIN SLICES CURED HAM
1 HANDFUL BABY MIXED GREENS

To make the Parmesan cream, in a saucepan, melt the butter, then add the flour and cook for 1 minute to make a roux. Gradually pour in the cream while whisking. Bring to a boil, then remove from the heat and stir in the Parmesan. Season with a pinch each of nutmeg, salt, and pepper.

Transfer to a dish and press plastic wrap directly onto the surface to prevent a skin from forming. Refrigerate for 1 hour.

To make the Parmesan craquelin, in the bowl of a stand mixer fitted with the paddle attachment, combine all ingredients until smooth. Roll the dough between two sheets of parchment paper to 1⁄12 inch (2 mm) thick, then refrigerate for 15 minutes.

To assemble the pastry, preheat the oven to 340°F (170°C) and line a baking sheet with parchment paper.

Pipe 8 evenly sized rounds of the Choux Pastry Dough, about 3 oz (80 g) each, onto the prepared baking sheet using a plain tip.

Cut out rounds of the chilled craquelin with a cutter the same size as the choux and place one on top of each puff.

Bake for 25 minutes without opening the oven door. Then remove and let cool.

Slice each puff in half horizontally using a serrated knife.

Loosen the Parmesan cream by stirring with a spatula and pipe a small amount onto the bottom halves of each puff. Add a slice of ham and some greens on top of the cream. Add more Parmesan cream and place the top halves back on top to close the buns.

Red Berry Profiteroles

MAKES 4
PREP TIME: 10 MINUTES
COOK TIME: 25 MINUTES

PROFITEROLES
12 OZ (320 G) CHOUX PASTRY DOUGH (PAGE 35)
12 OZ (350 G) STRAWBERRY SORBET
3 ½ OZ (100 G) RASPBERRIES
3 ½ OZ (100 G) STRAWBERRIES

VANILLA CHANTILLY CREAM
1 ¼ CUPS (300 ML) HEAVY CREAM
1 TBSP SUGAR
SEEDS OF 1 VANILLA BEAN

To bake the choux, preheat the oven to 340°F (170°C) and line a baking sheet with parchment paper.

Pipe 4 evenly sized rounds of the Choux Pastry Dough, about 3 oz (80 g) each, onto the prepared baking sheet using a plain tip.

Bake for 25 minutes without opening the oven door. Then remove and let cool.

To make the vanilla chantilly cream, in the bowl of a stand mixer fitted with the whisk attachment, whip the cream, sugar, and vanilla seeds until soft peaks form.

Slice each choux in half horizontally with a serrated knife, leaving one side intact to create a hinge. Add a generous scoop of strawberry sorbet and close the sandwich. Pipe the chantilly cream on top and scatter with fresh berries. Serve immediately.

Vanilla & Chocolate Profiteroles

SERVES 4
PREP TIME: 15 MINUTES
COOK TIME: 30 MINUTES

PROFITEROLES
12 OZ (320 G) CHOUX PASTRY DOUGH (PAGE 35)
12 OZ (350 G) VANILLA ICE CREAM
7 OZ (200 G) CHOCOLATE GRANOLA

CHOCOLATE SAUCE
7 OZ (210 ML) WHOLE MILK
3½ TBSP HEAVY CREAM
1 VANILLA BEAN, SPLIT AND SCRAPED
1 TBSP SUGAR
3½ OZ (100 G) CHOCOLATE, CHOPPED OR CHIPS

To bake the choux, preheat the oven to 340°F (170°C) and line a baking sheet with parchment paper.

Pipe 4 evenly sized rounds of the Choux Pastry Dough, about 3 oz (80 g) each, onto the prepared baking sheet using a plain tip.

Bake for 25 minutes without opening the oven door. Then remove and let cool.

To make the chocolate sauce, in a medium saucepan, heat the milk and cream with the vanilla bean and seeds. Mix to combine and keep warm.

In a separate heavy saucepan, add the sugar and cook over moderate heat until the sugar begins to liquify.

Once it begins to caramelize, stir gently and carefully add the hot milk mixture (remove the vanilla pod first).

Place the chocolate into a heatproof bowl and pour the hot milk-caramel mixture over it, a third at a time, whisking until smooth.

Slice each choux in half horizontally with a serrated knife without cutting all the way through. Fill with a generous scoop of vanilla ice cream and close the sandwich.

Pour the warm chocolate sauce over the top and onto the plate, then sprinkle with the chocolate granola. Serve immediately.

Vanilla Sweet Pastry Dough

Delicious and quick to prepare, Vanilla Sweet Pastry Dough can be used in desserts such as Quick Strawberry Tart (page 48), Buckwheat Chocolate Tart (page 53), and Sliced Almond Florentines (page 149).

MAKES 1 LB (450 G)
PREP TIME: 10 MINUTES
CHILL TIME: 8 HOURS

9 TBSP BUTTER, ROOM TEMPERATURE
⅔ CUP (80 G) POWDERED SUGAR
¼ CUP (27 G) ALMOND FLOUR
1 EGG
1 TSP VANILLA EXTRACT
1 ¾ CUPS (216 G) ALL-PURPOSE FLOUR

In the bowl of a stand mixer fitted with the paddle attachment, cream together the butter, powdered sugar, and almond flour.

Add the egg and vanilla, and mix until smooth. Gradually incorporate the all-purpose flour a third at a time, mixing just until combined. Do not overwork the dough.

Shape the dough into a ball, flatten to about ¾ inch (2 cm) thick, wrap in plastic, and refrigerate for 8 hours.

Quick Strawberry Tart

With strawberries mixed into whipped cream, this tart comes together easily and is so good you'll make it again and again.

SERVES 6
PREP TIME: 15 MINUTES
BAKE TIME: 20 MINUTES

VANILLA SWEET PASTRY DOUGH (PAGE 45), CHILLED, OR 1 PREBAKED 9-INCH (22-CM) TART SHELL

⅔ CUP (150 G) CRÈME FRAÎCHE

⅔ CUP (150 G) FAT-FREE FROMAGE BLANC OR GREEK YOGURT

1 TBSP SUGAR

SEEDS OF 1 VANILLA BEAN

ZEST FROM 1 LIME

1 LB (450 G) STRAWBERRIES, DIVIDED, HULLED, AND HALVED

3 ½ OZ (100 G) VANILLA CRUMBLE (PAGE 50)

1 CUP CRUMBLED VANILLA MERINGUE (PAGE 56), OPTIONAL

Preheat the oven to 320°F (160°C).

If using Vanilla Sweet Pastry Dough, grease a 9-inch (22-cm) tart pan. Remove the dough from the refrigerator and roll the dough out to ⅛ to 1⁄12 inch (2 to 3 mm) thick on a floured surface. Transfer the dough to the tart pan and blind bake for 20 minutes. Cool completely before filling.

In the bowl of a stand mixer fitted with the whisk attachment, combine the crème fraîche, fromage blanc, sugar, vanilla seeds, and lime zest. Whip until soft peaks form. Fold in half of the strawberries. Fill the tart shell with the mixture.

Sprinkle with the Vanilla Crumble, top with the remaining strawberries, and add meringue pieces, if desired.

Vanilla Crumble

I use this crumble to finish the Quick Strawberry Tart *(page 48)**, but it's versatile enough to add to most fruit pies or tarts. It's a great make-ahead ingredient to have on hand, and it freezes well.*

MAKES 14 OZ (400 G)
PREP TIME: 10 MINUTES
BAKE TIME: 20 MINUTES

7 TBSP BUTTER
⅔ CUP (100 G) ALL-PURPOSE FLOUR
½ CUP (100 G) SUGAR
1 CUP (100 G) ALMOND FLOUR
1 PINCH FINE SALT
1 TSP VANILLA EXTRACT

Preheat the oven to 300°F (150°C) and line a baking sheet with parchment paper.

In the bowl of a stand mixer fitted with the paddle attachment, combine all of the ingredients.
Mix until the dough comes together.

Spread the crumble on the prepared baking sheet, breaking it up into small chunks and spacing them apart.

Bake for 20 minutes. Cool and store in an airtight container at room temperature for up to 1 month.

Babas

Babas are small yeasted cakes that are left to dry out a bit before being soaked in flavorful syrup. One of the most common varieties found in pastry cases is the rum baba, but I like to make Bissap Baba (page 134), which flavors the cakes with tart hibiscus syrup.

MAKES 20 OZ (600 G)
PREP TIME: 15 MINUTES
PROOFING: 1 HOUR
BAKE TIME: 30 MINUTES
DRYING TIME: AT LEAST 24 HOURS

2 ¼ CUPS (280 G) FLOUR
1 TSP FINE SALT
1 ½ TBSP SUGAR
3 EGGS
¼ CUP (60 ML) MILK
1 TBSP FRESH BAKER'S YEAST OR 1 ½ TSP ACTIVE DRY YEAST
4 ½ TBSP BUTTER, SOFTENED

In the bowl of a stand mixer fitted with the paddle attachment, combine the flour, salt, sugar, and eggs. Mix until incorporated, about 2 minutes.

Meanwhile, warm the milk in a glass container in the microwave. Add the yeast and set aside to bloom, about 5 minutes.

Gradually pour the warm milk and yeast into the dough while mixing on medium speed. This develops the gluten and will help the babas keep their shape after soaking.

Once the dough pulls away from the sides of the bowl and looks smooth, add the butter and 2 tsp of water. Mix for 5 more minutes until the dough pulls away again.

Weigh out 1-oz (30-g) portions of dough and add them to silicone half-sphere molds (there's no need to grease the silicone molds).

Preheat the oven to 120°F (50°C), then turn it off and place the molds inside to proof for 1 hour.

Remove from the oven, then preheat to 360°F (180°C). Bake for 30 minutes. Immediately after baking, remove the babas from the molds and cool on a wire rack. Let them air-dry for at least 24 hours.

Buckwheat Chocolate Tart

SERVES 6 TO 8
PREP TIME: 20 MINUTES
CHILL TIME: 40 MINUTES
BAKE TIME: 25 MINUTES

BUTTER FOR GREASING THE PAN
9 OZ (250 G) VANILLA SWEET PASTRY DOUGH (PAGE 45)
⅓ CUP (80 ML) WHOLE MILK
¼ CUP (60 ML) HEAVY CREAM
2 TBSP HONEY
6 OZ (180 G) DARK CHOCOLATE, FINELY CHOPPED
7 OZ (200 G) BUCKWHEAT-ALMOND PRALINÉ (PAGE 153)
1 PINCH FLEUR DE SEL
2 PINCHES TOASTED BUCKWHEAT OR KASHA*

Grease a 9-inch (22-cm) tart pan with butter. Roll out the dough to ⅛ to 1⁄12 inch (2 to 3 mm) thick on a floured surface. Transfer the dough to the tart pan and prick the base with a fork. Refrigerate for 20 minutes.

Preheat the oven to 320°F (160°C).

Bake the tart shell for 20 minutes until evenly golden. Remove from the oven and cool.

To make the ganache, add the milk, cream, and honey to a medium saucepan. Bring to a boil and remove from the heat. Place the chopped chocolate in a medium bowl and pour the milk mixture over the chocolate a third at a time, stirring between each addition to create a smooth emulsion.

To assemble, spread the praliné in the cooled tart shell. Pour the still-warm ganache over the top. Sprinkle with fleur de sel and toasted buckwheat.

Chill the tart in the refrigerator for 20 minutes to set the ganache, then let it sit at room temperature until ready to serve.

* *If using raw buckwheat, lightly toast for 1 hour before beginning the recipe.*

Red Berry Pavlova

Usually, vanilla extract can be substituted for vanilla powder, but not in this recipe. The powder, which can be purchased online, keeps the sugar dry which is critical to keeping the pavlova airy and crisp. It's best to assemble the pavlova shortly before serving, as the meringue quickly absorbs moisture in the fridge. The vanilla meringue in this recipe can also be repurposed as decoration for the Quick Strawberry Tart (page 48).

SERVES 6 TO 8
PREP TIME: 40 MINUTES
BAKE TIME: 1 HOUR

VANILLA MERINGUE

3 EGG WHITES

¾ CUP (180 G) SUGAR, DIVIDED

1 TSP POWDERED VANILLA

WHIPPED CREAM

1 ¼ CUPS (300 ML) HEAVY CREAM

1 TBSP SUGAR

SEEDS OF 1 VANILLA BEAN

TOPPINGS

½ PINT STRAWBERRIES, HULLED AND HALVED

½ PINT BLUEBERRIES

½ PINT RASPBERRIES

3 TO 5 BASIL LEAVES

To make the vanilla meringue, preheat the oven to 250°F (120°C). In the bowl of a stand mixer fitted with the whisk attachment, beat the egg whites on medium speed for 20 minutes, gradually adding half of the sugar a third at a time.

In a separate bowl, mix the remaining sugar with the powdered vanilla.

Once the meringue is smooth and glossy and the first half of the sugar has dissolved, fold in the vanilla sugar by hand using a spatula.

Draw an 8-inch (20-cm) circle on a sheet of parchment paper, flip it over, and place it on a baking sheet. Pipe small rounds of meringue along the edge of the circle, then fill the center by piping in a spiral. Pipe a few extra small meringue rounds for decoration. Bake immediately—this helps the vanilla sugar stay dry and the meringue crisp—for 1 hour.

To make the whipped cream, in the bowl of a stand mixer fitted with the whisk attachment, whip the cream with the sugar and vanilla seeds. Whip to soft peaks, then finish tightening the texture by whisking by hand.

Transfer to a piping bag with the tip cut on a slant.

To assemble, pipe a base layer of whipped cream in the center of the meringue. Add the strawberries, packing them closely. Pipe more whipped cream over the top in a rustic, messy style.

Top with more fruit, a few basil leaves, and the decorative meringue rounds.

2

VEGETABLES

There's simply nothing like cooking with fresh vegetables tended by hand—either yours or a local farmer's. And there are few things more rewarding than garden surpluses turned into preserves that feed us year-round.

Zero-Waste Vegetable Broth

MAKES 2 QUARTS
PREP TIME: 10 MINUTES
COOK TIME: 1 HOUR

PEA PODS
CARROT TOPS
ONION PEELS
ZUCCHINI TRIMMINGS
FENNEL CORES AND PEELS
OLIVE OIL

In a large pot, sauté all of the vegetable scraps in a drizzle of olive oil for 5 minutes.

Add 2 quarts of water and bring to a boil. Cover and simmer over low heat for 1 hour.

Strain through a fine mesh sieve, pressing lightly to extract the juices. Pour into storage containers and use immediately or freeze.

Jarred Vegetables

When the garden overproduces, canning is a great way to preserve the harvest. The listed amounts of aromatics are for one jar. Adjust as needed based on your vegetable quantities.

MAKES 5 ASSORTED 1-QUART (1-L) JARS
PREP TIME: 30 MINUTES
CHILL TIME: 1 HOUR

4 QT (4 L) ZERO-WASTE VEGETABLE BROTH (PAGE 63)

⅓ CUP (80 G) SALT

GREEN BEANS

SALT

1 LB (450 G) GREEN BEANS, TRIMMED

1 BUNCH CURLY PARSLEY, CHOPPED

1 ONION, SLICED

RED ONIONS

3 RED ONIONS, SLICED

1 SPRIG SAGE

EGGPLANT

2 EGGPLANTS, CUT INTO ¾-BY-4 INCH (2-BY-10 CM) PIECES

1 BUNCH BASIL

ZUCCHINI

2 ZUCCHINI, CUT INTO ¾-BY-4 INCH (2-BY-10 CM) PIECES

1 SPRIG ROSEMARY

CARROTS

4 CARROTS, PEELS ON AND CUT INTO ¾-BY-4 INCH (2-BY-10 CM) PIECES

1 SPRIG THYME

1 BAY LEAF

Sterilize 5 heatproof quart (liter) jars (or as many as you're making).

In a large pot, combine the broth with the salt over low heat and mix until the salt has dissolved. Remove from the heat to cool to room temperature, then chill in the refrigerator for 1 hour.

Green Beans

In a saucepan of boiling salted water, blanch the green beans for 5 minutes, then plunge into ice water to preserve the bright green color.

Pack tightly into the jar along with the parsley and onion leaving ¾ inch (2 cm) of headspace. Pour in the cold broth to cover.

Red Onions

Pack the onions into the jar up to ¾ inch (2 cm) from the top. Add the sprig of sage and cover with cold broth.

Eggplant

Pack the eggplant into the jar up to ¾ inch (2 cm) from the top. Add the basil. Pour in the cold broth to cover.

Zucchini

Pack the zucchini into the jar up to ¾ inch (2 cm) from the top. Add the rosemary and top with the cold broth.

Carrots

Pack the carrots into the jar up to ¾ inch (2 cm) from the top and add the thyme and bay leaf. Pour in the cold broth to cover.

Seal the jars and place them in a pot lined with a kitchen towel. Fill the pot with water to three-quarters full (the jars should be fully submerged). Bring to a boil and cook for 1 hour to gently confit. Remove and turn the jars upside down to cool. If any lid hasn't sealed, refrigerate and consume within 2 weeks.

Slow-Roasted Cherry Tomatoes

These summer beauties are perfect on toasted bread, in salads, or on pizza.

MAKES ONE 8-OZ (250-ML) JAR
PREP TIME: 25 MINUTES
COOK TIME: 1 HOUR

12 OZ (350 G) WHOLE CHERRY TOMATOES, HALVED
3 GARLIC CLOVES, PEELED AND CRUSHED
1 SPRIG THYME
1 BAY LEAF
OLIVE OIL

Sterilize a heatproof half-pint (250-ml) jar.

Scoop the seeds out of the tomatoes with a small spoon and discard.

In the jar, add the tomatoes, crushed garlic, thyme, and bay leaf. Fill with olive oil to cover up to ¾ inch (2 cm) from the top.

Seal the jar and place it in a pot lined with a kitchen towel. Fill the pot with water to three-quarters full (the jar should be fully submerged). Bring to a boil and cook for 1 hour to gently confit. Remove and turn the jar upside down to cool.

Store sealed at room temperature for up to 6 months and in the refrigerator for 2 months after opening.

Roasted Pepper Spread

Eat this flavorful dip on toasted bread, in a sandwich, or as part of a veggie platter.

MAKES ONE 8-OZ (250-ML) JAR
PREP TIME: 15 MINUTES
COOK TIME: 40 MINUTES

1 RED BELL PEPPER, CHOPPED
1 YELLOW BELL PEPPER, CHOPPED
1 RED ONION, CHOPPED
14 OZ (400 G) HEIRLOOM TOMATOES, CHOPPED
3 GARLIC CLOVES, CRUSHED
1 SPRIG THYME
WHOLE BLACK PEPPERCORNS
SALT
OLIVE OIL
3 ½ OZ (100 G) RAW ALMONDS

Preheat the oven to 430°F (220°C) and line a baking sheet with parchment paper.

Place the peppers, onion, tomatoes, garlic, thyme, and peppercorns on the prepared baking sheet. Sprinkle with a pinch of salt and drizzle with olive oil.

Roast for 25 to 30 minutes until nicely browned. Turn off the oven and add the almonds to the baking sheet to lightly toast, about 10 minutes. Remove from the oven and let everything cool to room temperature.

Blend the vegetables and almonds in a food processor with another drizzle of olive oil until smooth.

Store in an airtight jar in the fridge for up to 1 week.

Roasted Summer Vegetables

MAKES ONE 1-QUART (1-L) JAR
PREP TIME: 20 MINUTES
COOK TIME: 1 HOUR 30 MINUTES

2 RED BELL PEPPERS, QUARTERED
2 RED ONIONS, CUT INTO WEDGES
2 ZUCCHINI, CUT INTO THICK SLICES
1 EGGPLANT, CUT INTO THICK SLICES
OLIVE OIL
SALT
WHOLE BLACK PEPPERCORNS
2 TBSP WHITE VINEGAR

Sterilize a heatproof quart (liter) jar. Preheat the oven to 430°F (220°C) and line a baking sheet with parchment paper.

Spread the peppers, onions, zucchini, and eggplant onto the baking sheet, drizzle with olive oil, and sprinkle with salt. Roast for 20 to 30 minutes until lightly browned.

Let cool, then layer the vegetables in the jar with a few peppercorns. Cover with olive oil and vinegar up to ¾ inch (2 cm) from the top.

For long-term storage, seal the jar and place it in a pot lined with a kitchen towel. Fill the pot with water to three-quarters full (the jar should be fully submerged). Bring to a boil and cook for 1 hour. Remove and turn the jar upside down to cool. If the lid hasn't sealed, refrigerate and consume within 2 weeks.

Store at room temperature for up to 6 months. Refrigerate after opening for up to 2 months.

Quick Tomato Sauce

MAKES ABOUT 1 ½ CUPS
PREP TIME: 15 MINUTES
COOK TIME: 30 MINUTES

5 VINE TOMATOES
OLIVE OIL
SALT
1 RED ONION, FINELY DICED
2 GARLIC CLOVES, MINCED
2 PINCHES HERBES DE PROVENCE

Preheat the oven to 430°F (220°C) and line a baking sheet with parchment paper.

Place the whole tomatoes with vines on the baking sheet, drizzle with olive oil, and sprinkle with salt. Roast for 20 minutes.

In a saucepan, sauté the onion and garlic in olive oil until lightly golden.

Add the roasted tomatoes (discard the vines), along with the herbes de Provence.

Break down the tomatoes with a spatula and simmer over low heat for 5 minutes. Add a splash of water if needed to help them cook down.

Blend the sauce with an immersion blender.

Use immediately or pour it piping hot into a sterilized jar and close. Turn upside down to cool and seal.

Sauce keeps for 3 to 4 months at room temperature and 2 weeks in the fridge once opened.

Eggplant & Hazelnut Dip

SERVES 4 TO 5 AS AN APPETIZER
PREP TIME: 15 MINUTES
COOK TIME: 40 MINUTES

6 EGGPLANTS OR ABOUT 2 ½ LBS (1,125 G) COOKED FLESH
1 ¾ OZ (50 G) HAZELNUTS, CRUSHED, PLUS EXTRA FOR GARNISH
½ CUP (120 G) BUTTER
10 WHOLE BLACK PEPPERCORNS
2 TBSP LEMON JUICE
1 PINCH SICHUAN PEPPER
1 PINCH SALT
1 SHALLOT, FINELY CHOPPED

Preheat the oven to 430°F (220°C) and line a baking sheet with parchment paper.

Place the whole eggplants on the prepared baking sheet. Roast for 30 minutes. Turn off the oven and add the hazelnuts to the baking sheet and toast for 10 minutes. Remove from the oven.

Once the eggplants are cool enough to handle, peel and discard the skin, then transfer the flesh to a blender.

In a saucepan over medium heat, brown the butter. Once the milk solids begin to caramelize, add the hazelnuts and peppercorns.

Reserving a small amount of browned butter for serving, pour the mixture over the eggplant flesh. Add the lemon juice, Sichuan pepper, and salt, then blend until smooth.

Stir in the chopped shallot by hand.

Serve warm, topped with extra hazelnuts and the reserved browned butter.

Tarragon-Fermented Green Beans

Fermentation extends shelf life and enhances both flavor and nutritional value. Serve these beans in salads, maybe with fresh figs, walnuts, and more fresh tarragon. Since tap water often includes chlorine and fluoride, it's best to use spring water when fermenting.

MAKES ONE 8-OZ (250-ML) JAR
PREP TIME: 10 MINUTES
FERMENTATION: 3 TO 4 DAYS

1½ TSP SALT
1 CUP (240 ML) SPRING WATER
9 OZ (250 G) GREEN BEANS, TRIMMED
1 GARLIC CLOVE, CRUSHED
1 SPRIG TARRAGON
WHOLE BLACK PEPPERCORNS

In a small bowl, dissolve the salt in the spring water to make a brine.

Sterilize a jar by pouring boiling water into it and letting it sit for 5 minutes. Then pour out the water.

Pack the beans tightly into the jar with the garlic, tarragon, and a few peppercorns. Do not crush the beans. Pour in the brine, making sure the vegetables are fully submerged. Seal the jar and leave at room temperature to ferment. Once a day, briefly open the jar to release the built-up gas, then reseal. Repeat for 3 to 4 days.

After 3 days, taste. If you like the flavor, seal and transfer the jar to the refrigerator. If not, wait one more day. Once refrigerated, fermentation will slow significantly.

Store chilled for 3 to 6 months.

Carrot, Orange, Cumin & Vanilla Pickles

MAKES ONE 1-QUART (1-L) JAR
PREP TIME: 20 MINUTES
COOK TIME: 10 MINUTES
MARINATE: OVERNIGHT

1 LB (450 G) CARROTS
1 ORANGE
1 CUP (240 ML) WHITE VINEGAR
1 CUP (240 ML) FRESH ORANGE JUICE
1 VANILLA BEAN, SPLIT AND SCRAPED
2 TBSP HONEY
1 TSP SALT
2 TSP CUMIN SEEDS

Sterilize a heatproof quart (liter) jar. Wash the carrots with their skins on. Slice thinly on a slant with a knife or mandoline.

Using a peeler, remove strips of orange zest and cut them into very thin strips. Place the orange zest strips in a saucepan, cover with cold water, and bring to a boil to remove any bitterness. Repeat this blanching process a second time. Remove from the heat, drain the liquid, and add the carrots and zest to the jar.

In a large saucepan, bring the vinegar, orange juice, vanilla bean and seeds, honey, salt, and cumin seeds to a simmer.

Pour the hot liquid over the carrots and orange zest leaving ¾ inch (2 cm) of headspace. Refrigerate overnight.

The pickles are ready to eat the next day and can be stored in the refrigerator for up to 6 months.

Pickled Mushrooms

The wild mushroom season is short, and the best way to enjoy them all year long is to pickle them in brine.

MAKES THREE 8-OZ (250-ML) JARS
PREP TIME: 10 MINUTES
COOK TIME: 5 MINUTES

3 CUPS (720 ML) HIGH-QUALITY WHITE VINEGAR
⅔ CUP (150 G) SALT
⅓ CUP (90 G) SUGAR
1 ⅓ LBS (600 G) MUSHROOMS, DIVIDED, CLEANED, AND SLICED*
3 SPRIGS THYME, DIVIDED
3 BAY LEAVES, DIVIDED
1 TBSP WHOLE BLACK PEPPERCORNS, DIVIDED
1 TBSP MUSTARD SEEDS, DIVIDED

Sterilize 3 heatproof half-pint (250-ml) jars.

In a large saucepan, heat 3 cups (720 ml) of water along with the vinegar, salt, and sugar. Stir until dissolved.

Distribute 7 oz (200 g) of mushrooms into each sterilized jar. Add 1 thyme sprig, 1 bay leaf, 1 tsp black peppercorns, and 1 tsp mustard seeds per jar.

Pour in the hot brine until the mushrooms are fully submerged. Seal the jars and turn them upside down for 1 hour. Store in the fridge for up to 1 week.

For long-term storage, seal the jars by placing them in a pot lined with a kitchen towel. Fill the pot with water to three-quarters full (the jars should be fully submerged). Bring to a boil and cook for 1 hour. Remove and turn the jars upside down to cool. Store at room temperature for up to 6 months. If any lid hasn't sealed, refrigerate and consume within 2 weeks.

** Some mushrooms, such as morels, must be cooked before storing in brine.*

Homemade Ketchup

Of course this condiment goes great with fries, but also try it with red meat, in sandwiches, or with roasted vegetables like sweet potatoes.

MAKES ABOUT 2 CUPS (480 ML)
PREP TIME: 10 MINUTES
COOK TIME: 15 MINUTES

½ CUP (150 G) WILDFLOWER HONEY
2 TBSP BALSAMIC VINEGAR
2 ½ TBSP SOY SAUCE
1 ⅔ CUPS (400 ML) QUICK TOMATO SAUCE (PAGE 77)
1 PINCH GROUND BLACK PEPPER

In a saucepan over medium heat, bring the honey to a boil and cook until it turns a light amber caramel color. Deglaze with the vinegar and soy sauce. Add the tomato sauce and black pepper.

Simmer over low heat for 10 minutes to reduce slightly. Cover with a lid to prevent splattering. Once reduced, remove from heat and cool.

Store in the refrigerator for up to 3 months.

Homemade Barbecue Sauce

This versatile sauce makes a great marinade—slather pork ribs in this sauce and marinate for 24 hours. Then bake them at 350°F (175°C) for 1 ½ hours. It also works as a salad dressing base or a dipping sauce.

MAKES ABOUT 3 CUPS (720 ML)
PREP TIME: 15 MINUTES
COOK TIME: 20 MINUTES

2 RED BELL PEPPERS, THINLY SLICED
1 RED ONION, THINLY SLICED
2 GARLIC CLOVES, FINELY CHOPPED
1 TBSP FRESH GINGER, PEELED AND FINELY CHOPPED
OLIVE OIL
2 TBSP HONEY
3 TBSP SOY SAUCE
3 TBSP BALSAMIC VINEGAR
1 CUP (240 ML) QUICK TOMATO SAUCE (PAGE 77)
1 TBSP SMOKED PAPRIKA
10 BLACK PEPPERCORNS, CRUSHED
2 SPRIGS FRESH THYME
SALT

In a saucepan, sauté the peppers, onion, garlic, and ginger in olive oil until lightly golden. Add the honey and let it caramelize for 1 minute.

Deglaze with the soy sauce and balsamic vinegar. Add ⅓ cup (80 ml) of water, the tomato sauce, paprika, crushed peppercorns, and thyme. Simmer for 10 to 15 minutes over low heat to concentrate the flavors.

Remove the thyme sprigs. Blend with an immersion blender. Adjust seasoning with salt if needed. Refrigerate for up to 4 weeks.

Raspberry-Red Pepper Chutney

This chutney pairs beautifully with red meats. Its sweet and tangy flavor also elevates toasted bread for appetizers, and it earns its place alongside charcuterie or cheese boards.

MAKES ONE 8-OZ (250-ML) JAR
PREP TIME: 15 MINUTES
COOK TIME: 15 MINUTES

1 ½ LBS (675 G) RED BELL PEPPERS, DICED INTO ½-INCH (1-CM) CUBES
1 RED ONION, FINELY DICED
OLIVE OIL
½ CUP (100 G) SUGAR
3 TBSP SHERRY VINEGAR
9 OZ (250 G) RASPBERRIES, MASHED
1 PINCH GROUND CINNAMON
1 PINCH GROUND CUMIN

Sterilize a heatproof half-pint (250-ml) jar.

In a saucepan over medium heat, cook the peppers and onion in olive oil until lightly browned. Add the sugar, stir, and caramelize for 2 minutes. Deglaze with the sherry vinegar.

Add the raspberries and spices. Bring to a boil, then lower the heat and simmer for 5 minutes until the mixture reaches a jam-like consistency.

Transfer to the sterilized jar and refrigerate for up to 1 month.

Pierre Reboul's Pistou Soup

My friend Pierre Reboul is a pastry chef and a brilliant professional. We've shared many things, including the best pistou soup in the world. Pistou is the Provençal cousin of Italian pesto.

SERVES 5
PREP TIME: 30 MINUTES
COOK TIME: 1 HOUR 10 MINUTES

SOUP

7 OZ (200 G) POTATOES, PEELED AND DICED INTO ½-INCH (1-CM) CUBES

2 LARGE TOMATOES

OLIVE OIL

½ ONION, FINELY CHOPPED

14 OZ (400 G) SEMI-DRIED CRANBERRY BEANS

2 SPRIGS THYME

1 BAY LEAF

SALT AND PEPPER

1 ZUCCHINI (ABOUT 10 OZ/300 G), PEELED AND DICED INTO ½-INCH (1-CM) CUBES

3 OZ (80 G) GREEN BEANS, CHOPPED INTO ¾-INCH (2-CM) PIECES

3 OZ (80 G) YELLOW WAX BEANS, CHOPPED INTO ¾-INCH (2-CM) PIECES

3 OZ (80 G) FLAT BEANS, CHOPPED INTO ¾-INCH (2-CM) PIECES

PISTOU

2 BUNCHES BASIL, LEAVES ONLY

5 GARLIC CLOVES

SALT AND PEPPER

¾ CUP (180 ML) OLIVE OIL

ZEST AND JUICE FROM 1 LEMON

To make the soup, place the potatoes in a bowl of cool water. Fill a medium pot ⅔ full of water and bring to a boil. Blanch the tomatoes in boiling water for 20 seconds, then transfer to ice water and remove the skins. Seed and dice the tomatoes.

In a large pot, heat a drizzle of olive oil and sauté the onion until golden. Add the tomatoes and cook down for 5 minutes.

Add the cranberry beans, drained potatoes, thyme, bay leaf, salt, pepper, and 2 quarts (2 L) of fresh water. Simmer over low heat for 45 minutes.

Add the zucchini, green beans, yellow beans, and flat beans, and simmer for another 15 minutes. Then remove from the heat.

To make the pistou, using a mortar and pestle, crush the basil leaves with the garlic cloves and salt and pepper to taste. Add the olive oil, lemon zest, and lemon juice and incorporate into the mixture.

Stir ¼ cup (65 g) into the soup, and serve the rest at the table for guests to add as they wish.

Zucchini Tagliatelle with Ricotta

SERVES 4
PREP TIME: 15 MINUTES
COOK TIME: 5 MINUTES

2 GREEN ZUCCHINI
1 YELLOW ZUCCHINI
2 CUPS (480 ML) ZERO-WASTE VEGETABLE BROTH (PAGE 63)
JUICE FROM ½ LEMON
7 OZ (200 G) HOMEMADE CROUTONS (PAGE 195)
1 CUP (250 G) RICOTTA
OLIVE OIL
SALT AND PEPPER

Trim the ends of the zucchini and cut lengthwise into thick slabs using only the outer flesh (avoiding the seedy core). Then slice into ribbons with a mandoline. Arrange the ribbons in a deep platter or bowl.

Bring the broth to a boil in a saucepan, then ladle it over the zucchini ribbons. Add the lemon juice, then the croutons and ricotta. Season with a drizzle of olive oil, a pinch of salt, and a bit of pepper and serve.

Pascal Lafaye's Summer Vegetable Terrine

This dish reflects my friend Pascal perfectly–he's a butcher who loves vegetables. Paired with rustic bread or Homemade Melba Toast (page 196), this veggie-forward dish makes a wonderful summer appetizer.

MAKES ONE 4½-LB (2-KG) TERRINE
PREP TIME: 1 HOUR
COOK TIME: 30 MINUTES
CHILL TIME: OVERNIGHT

2 ZUCCHINI, SLICED 1 ¼ INCHES (3 CM) THICK
2 EGGPLANTS, SLICED 1 ¼ INCHES (3 CM) THICK
3 RED BELL PEPPERS, QUARTERED
1 RED ONION, QUARTERED
2 GARLIC CLOVES, UNPEELED
OLIVE OIL
FLEUR DE SEL
FRESHLY GROUND PEPPER
1 BUNCH BASIL
2 CUPS (480 ML) ZERO WASTE VEGETABLE BROTH (PAGE 63) OR 1 BOUILLON CUBE IN 2 CUPS (480 ML) WATER
2 TSP AGAR-AGAR

Preheat the oven to 400°F (200°C) and line a baking sheet with parchment paper.

Arrange the zucchini, eggplants, peppers, onion, and garlic on the prepared baking sheet. Drizzle with olive oil, season with pinches of fleur de sel and pepper, and roast for 30 minutes until lightly browned. Let cool.

Lightly oil an 8 ½ x 4 ½ inch (21.6 × 11.4 cm) metal or glass loaf pan.

Layer the vegetables, pressing down firmly and scattering basil leaves between layers.

Bring the broth to a boil with the agar-agar. Pour over the layered vegetables and refrigerate overnight.

The next day, run a knife along the edges of the pan to unmold.

Well-wrapped, the terrine will keep for up to 1 week in the fridge. Serve cold or room temperature.

3

FRUIT

For me, the arrival of fruit means the beginning of sunny days full of delicate strawberries, rhubarb, and cherries... So I seal the sunshine in a jar of jam to enjoy it all year long.

Wine-Poached Pears

Here's a recipe I used to make with Chef Pierre Reboul when we worked in the same restaurant. Think of this recipe like sangria.

MAKES ONE 1-QUART (1-L) JAR
PREP TIME: 15 MINUTES
INFUSE AND MACERATE: 2 HOURS
COOK TIME: 5 MINUTES
REST: 1 HOUR

1 ½ CUPS (360 ML) RED WINE, SUCH AS BEAUJOLAIS
2 ½ CUPS (500 G) SUGAR
1 ORANGE, QUARTERED WITH PEEL ON
1 LEMON, QUARTERED WITH PEEL ON
1 LIME, QUARTERED WITH PEEL ON
1 ½ OZ (40 G) FRESH GINGER, CRUSHED
5 OR 6 FIRM COMICE OR CONFERENCE PEARS, PEELED AND CORED

Sterilize a heatproof quart (liter) jar.

In a large saucepan, heat the wine, sugar, and 1 ½ cups (360 ml) of water.

Add the orange, lemon, lime, and ginger to the saucepan and bring to a boil. Remove from the heat and infuse for 1 hour.

Strain the syrup, return to the saucepan, and bring it back to a boil. Remove from the heat and add the pears. Let them soak for 1 hour, turning them every 20 minutes.

Transfer the pears to the sterilized jar. Boil the syrup again and pour it into the jar. Seal by turning the jar upside down for 1 hour to create a vacuum.

Store for up to 6 months at room temperature. Refrigerate after opening.

Poached Pears with Sweet Clover

Herbaceous sweet clover is often planted at the base of certain wheat crops to help structure their growth. Sweet clover is increasingly being used as an ingredient, either in plant form for its grassy flavor (which is reminiscent of hay) or in seed form for a taste similar to tonka beans.

MAKES ONE 1-QUART (1-L) JAR
PREP TIME: 20 MINUTES
INFUSION AND MACERATION: 1 HOUR 15 MINUTES
COOK TIME: 25 MINUTES

½ OZ (15 G) DRIED SWEET CLOVER OR 1 GRATED TONKA BEAN
2 ½ CUPS (500 G) SUGAR, DIVIDED
1 VANILLA BEAN, SPLIT AND SCRAPED
5 OR 6 FIRM PEARS, PEELED AND CORED

Sterilize a heatproof quart (liter) jar. Preheat the oven to 320°F (160°C) and line a baking sheet with parchment paper.

Toast the sweet clover for 15 minutes, or dry-toast the clover in a skillet over low heat until lightly golden.

In a saucepan, add half the sugar and make a dry caramel by cooking over moderate heat until the sugar begins to liquify and turn light amber, about 355°F (180°C). Carefully deglaze with 3 ¼ cups (780 ml) water. Once the caramel is fully dissolved, add the remaining sugar, the vanilla bean and seeds, and toasted sweet clover. Bring to a boil, then remove from the heat and let infuse for 15 minutes.

Place the pears in the hot syrup off the heat and let them soak for 1 hour, turning every 20 minutes.

Transfer the pears to the sterilized jar. Bring the syrup to a boil and pour it over the pears. Seal the jar by turning it upside down until cool to create a vacuum.

Store for up to 6 months at room temperature. Refrigerate after opening.

Red Berry & Cinnamon Jam

You can reduce the sugar content, but the shelf life will be shorter.

MAKES ABOUT SIX 10-OZ (300-ML) JARS
PREP TIME: 10 MINUTES
MACERATION: 2 HOURS
COOK TIME: 15 MINUTES

3 ½ CUPS (700 G) SUGAR
1 TBSP PECTIN
1 LB (450 G) STRAWBERRIES, HULLED AND HALVED
9 OZ (250 G) RASPBERRIES
9 OZ (250 G) BLUEBERRIES
1 VANILLA BEAN, SPLIT AND SCRAPED
1 CINNAMON STICK

Sterilize 6 heatproof 10-oz jars.

In a large bowl, whisk together the sugar and pectin. Add the strawberries, raspberries, and blueberries to the bowl, stir gently, and let macerate for 2 hours.

Transfer the mixture to a large pot and add the vanilla bean and seeds and the cinnamon stick. Gently cook over low heat, stirring with a wooden spoon until the fruit breaks down. Bring to a full boil and cook for 5 minutes. Skim the surface to remove any foam.

Remove the vanilla bean and cinnamon stick. Transfer to the sterilized jars. Seal the jars by placing them in a pot lined with a kitchen towel. Fill the pot with water to three-quarters full (the jars should be fully submerged). Bring to a boil and cook for 1 hour. Remove and turn the jars upside down to cool. Store at room temperature for up to 6 months. If any lid hasn't sealed, refrigerate and consume within 2 weeks.

Apricot-Rosemary Jam

Much like the previous recipe, you can reduce the sugar content, but the shelf life will be shorter.

MAKES ABOUT SIX 10-OZ (300-ML) JARS
PREP TIME: 10 MINUTES
COOK TIME: 15 MINUTES

3 ½ CUPS (700 G) SUGAR
1 TSP PECTIN
2.2 LBS (1 KG) APRICOTS, PITTED AND QUARTERED
1 VANILLA BEAN, SPLIT AND SCRAPED
1 SPRIG ROSEMARY

Sterilize 6 heatproof 10-oz jars.

In a small bowl, whisk the sugar with the pectin.

In a large saucepan, combine the apricots with the sugar mixture. Add the vanilla bean and seeds and the rosemary. Cook gently over low heat, stirring regularly.

Once the apricots soften, remove the vanilla bean and blend slightly with an immersion blender. Bring to a full boil and cook for 5 minutes. Skim the surface to remove any foam.

Transfer to the sterilized jars. Seal the jars by placing them in a pot lined with a kitchen towel. Fill the pot with water to three-quarters full (the jars should be fully submerged). Bring to a boil and cook for 1 hour. Remove and turn the jars upside down to cool. Store at room temperature for up to 6 months. If any lid hasn't sealed, refrigerate and consume within 2 weeks.

Green Tomato, Raspberry & Mint Jam

Growing up, when the tomatoes stopped ripening at the end of summer, my grandfather—who was a farmer—would harvest them green to make this tangy jam.

MAKES FIVE 8-OZ (250-ML) JARS
PREP TIME: 10 MINUTES
COOK TIME: 10 MINUTES

3 CUPS (600 G) SUGAR
1 ½ TSP PECTIN
2.2 LBS (1 KG) GREEN OR GREEN ZEBRA TOMATOES, DICED
1 VANILLA BEAN, SPLIT AND SCRAPED
3 SPRIGS FRESH MINT, CHOPPED
3 ½ OZ (100 G) FRESH RASPBERRIES

Sterilize 5 heatproof 8-oz jars.

In a large bowl, combine the sugar and pectin. Add tomatoes and toss. Let rest for 10 minutes.

Transfer to a large saucepan, add the vanilla bean and seeds, and bring to a boil. Cook for 10 minutes. Add the mint and raspberries, then bring to a boil again.

Remove the vanilla bean and pour into the sterilized jars. Seal the jars by placing them in a pot lined with a kitchen towel. Fill the pot with water to three-quarters full (the jars should be fully submerged). Bring to a boil and cook for 1 hour. Remove and turn the jars upside down to cool and seal. Store at room temperature for up to 6 months. If any lid hasn't sealed, refrigerate and consume within 2 weeks.

Green Rhubarb Jam

Rhubarb is one of my favorite ingredients because it's the first sign of warm weather. You may use jam sugar if available. As always, you can reduce the sugar content, but the jam won't keep as long.

MAKES ABOUT SIX 10-OZ (300-ML) JARS
PREP TIME: 10 MINUTES
COOK TIME: 10 MINUTES

1 TSP PECTIN
3 ½ CUPS (700 G) SUGAR
2.2 LBS (1 KG) GREEN RHUBARB, PEELED AND CUT INTO ¾-INCH (2-CM) CHUNKS
1 VANILLA BEAN, SPLIT AND SCRAPED
1 WHOLE CLOVE

Sterilize 6 heatproof 10-oz jars.

In a small bowl, whisk the pectin into the sugar. In a large saucepan, combine the rhubarb, sugar mixture, vanilla bean and seeds, and clove.

Cook gently over low heat, stirring often. Once the rhubarb breaks down, bring to a full boil and cook for 5 minutes.

Remove vanilla bean and transfer to the sterilized jars. Seal the jars by placing them in a pot lined with a kitchen towel. Fill the pot with water to three-quarters full (the jars should be fully submerged). Bring to a boil and cook for 1 hour. Remove and turn the jars upside down to cool and seal. Store at room temperature for up to 6 months. If any lid hasn't sealed, refrigerate and consume within 2 weeks.

Prune & Almond Hummus

I love prunes, and I'm always a fan of the sweet-and-savory balance.

SERVES 4 TO 5 AS AN APPETIZER
PREP TIME: 15 MINUTES
SOAKING: 15 MINUTES
COOK TIME: 20 MINUTES

1 ½ OZ (35 G) WILDFLOWER HONEY
6 ½ OZ (180 G) PITTED PRUNES
2 ½ OZ (70 G) RAW ALMONDS
3 ½ TBSP OLIVE OIL
5 TO 6 BLACK PEPPERCORNS
1 LB (450 G) COOKED CHICKPEAS, DRAINED
SALT

In a saucepan, bring ½ cup (120 ml) water and the honey to a boil. Add the prunes, then remove from the heat and let soak for 15 minutes.

Preheat the oven to 320°F (160°C), lay the almonds on a baking sheet in an even layer, and toast them for 20 minutes. (Alternatively, you can toast the almonds in a skillet over medium heat.)

In a blender or food processor, blend the warm almonds into a paste. Add the honey-soaked prunes, their liquid, and the olive oil. Then add the peppercorns, chickpeas, and a pinch of salt. Blend until very smooth.

Store in the fridge for up to 1 week.

Chef Coly's Armagnac Prunes

This recipe is from my friend Didier Coly, who is a cook with a serious sweet tooth.

MAKES ONE 1-QUART (1-L) JAR
PREP TIME: 10 MINUTES
SOAKING: OVERNIGHT
COOK TIME: 10 MINUTES

1 LB (450 G) AGEN PRUNES* WITH PITS
1 ½ CUPS (360 ML) ARMAGNAC
½ CUP (100 G) GRANULATED SUGAR
1 VANILLA BEAN, SPLIT AND SCRAPED
1 LEMON, QUARTERED WITH PEEL

Sterilize 1 heatproof quart (liter) jar.

Soak the prunes in water overnight.

The next day, drain the prunes. In a saucepan, bring the Armagnac, sugar, vanilla bean and seeds, and lemon to a boil. Lower the heat and simmer for 10 minutes. Remove from the heat and don't strain.

Place the prunes in the sterilized jar and pour the hot syrup over them. Seal and invert for 1 hour to create a vacuum. Store at room temperature.

** Agen prunes with pits can be found in specialty stores and purchased online.*

Pickled Unripe Fruit

These recipes are perfect for using up end-of-season fruit that won't ripen in time. Serve the pickles in salads and sandwiches, alongside charcuterie boards, and more.

MAKES ONE 24-OZ (700-ML) JAR PER FRUIT TYPE
PREP TIME: 10 MINUTES
COOK TIME: 5 MINUTES
REST: OVERNIGHT

Cinnamon-Apple Pickles

2 GREEN APPLES, CORED AND THINLY SLICED

1 ¼ CUPS (300 ML) WATER OR APPLE-GINGER DRINK (PAGE 135)

½ CUP (100 G) LIGHT BROWN SUGAR

¾ CUP (180 ML) APPLE CIDER VINEGAR

1 CINNAMON STICK

Lemongrass-Pear Pickles

A FEW DROPS LEMON JUICE

2 UNDERRIPE PEARS (CONFERENCE, COMICE, OR WILLIAMS), THINLY SLICED

½ CUP (100 G) SUGAR

¾ CUP (180 ML) RICE OR WHITE VINEGAR

1 STALK LEMONGRASS, ROUGHLY CHOPPED

Cinnamon-Apple Pickles

Sterilize 1 heatproof 24-oz jar.

Place the apple slices in the sterilized glass jar.

In a saucepan, bring the water (or Apple-Ginger Drink), brown sugar, vinegar, and cinnamon stick to a boil. Pour the hot liquid over the apples to cover.

Seal immediately and invert until cooled. Let rest overnight before eating. Refrigerate for 2 to 3 weeks.

Lemongrass-Pear Pickles

Sterilize 1 heatproof 24-oz jar.

Drizzle the lemon juice over the pears to prevent browning, then place the pears in the sterilized jar.

In a saucepan, bring 1 ¼ cups (300 ml) water, sugar, vinegar, and lemongrass to a boil.

Pour the hot liquid into the jar to cover. Seal and invert until cooled.

Store in a cool, dark place for up to 6 months. Refrigerate after opening.

Bissap

This refreshing hibiscus tea can be poured over ice, diluted with fizzy water, or added to cocktails.

MAKES 1 QUART (1 L)
PREP TIME: 5 MINUTES
COOK TIME: 5 MINUTES
INFUSE: 1 HOUR

¾ OZ (20 G) DRIED HIBISCUS
¾ OZ (20 G) FRESH GINGER, CRUSHED WITH SKIN ON
3 TBSP GRANULATED SUGAR
4 SPRIGS FRESH MINT

In a medium saucepan, combine 1 quart (1 L) of water and the hibiscus, ginger, and sugar.

Bring to a boil, then remove from the heat and add the mint. Let infuse at room temperature for 1 hour.

Strain and transfer to a bottle. Store chilled for up to 2 weeks.

Bissap Baba

In this dessert, small yeasted cakes called babas are soaked in a beautiful and tart hibiscus (bissap) syrup.

MAKES 6
PREP TIME: 30 MINUTES
COOK TIME: 10 MINUTES
INFUSE: OVERNIGHT
SOAKING: 1 HOUR

¾ OZ (20 G) FRESH GINGER, PEELED AND CRUSHED
2 CUPS (430 G) SUGAR, PLUS 1 TBSP
¾ OZ (20 G) DRIED HIBISCUS
¾ OZ (20 G) FRESH MINT
6 BABAS, BAKED AND DRIED (PAGE 51)
¾ CUP (180 ML) HEAVY CREAM
ZEST FROM 1 LEMON

In a medium saucepan, bring 1 quart (1 L) water to a boil. Add the ginger, 2 cups (430 g) of sugar, and hibiscus. Remove from the heat, add the fresh mint, and refrigerate overnight.

The next day, strain the bissap into a saucepan and gently warm to 115°F (50°C).

Take the bissap off the heat and pour into a large baking dish. Soak the babas in the warm infusion for 1 hour, turning every 20 minutes. They will double in size and should be fully saturated.

In a stand mixer fitted with the whisk attachment, whip the cream, 1 tbsp sugar, and lemon zest. Whip to soft peaks. Spoon the whipped cream over the soaked babas and serve.

Apple-Ginger Drink

This tonic is a great way to make use of the apple scraps from recipes like Cinnamon-Apple Pickles (page 128) and Almond Milk Porridge (page 172)

MAKES 1 QUART (1 L)
PREP TIME: 10 MINUTES
COOK TIME: 10 MINUTES
INFUSE: OVERNIGHT

1 LB (450 G) PEELS AND CORES FROM BELLE DE BOSKOOP APPLE OR OTHER TART VARIETY

1 LEMON, HALVED

¼ CUP (50 G) SUGAR

1 OZ (30 G) FRESH GINGER, PEELED AND CRUSHED

In a large saucepan, combine 1 quart (1 L) water, apple scraps, and lemon halves (do not squeeze).

Bring to a boil with the lid on, then remove from the heat. Let infuse at room temperature overnight.

The next day, strain and discard the solids. Add the sugar and ginger. Bring to a boil again.

Pour into a sterilized glass bottle, seal, and invert for 1 hour to cool and seal. Refrigerate and consume within 2 weeks.

Best served chilled, though it also makes a lovely warm infusion.

4

GRAINS, NUTS & SEEDS

This chapter brings together everything that delivers crunch, roasted flavors, and toasted notes.

Cumin-Spiced Roasted Nuts

MAKES 1 LB (450 G)
PREP TIME: 10 MINUTES
BAKE TIME: 30 MINUTES

1 ¼ CUPS (250 G) RAW HAZELNUTS
1 ¼ CUPS (250 G) RAW ALMONDS
1 EGG WHITE
½ TSP SALT
1 TBSP LIGHT BROWN SUGAR
2 TSP GROUND CUMIN

Preheat the oven to 320°F (160°C). Line a baking sheet with parchment paper.

In a large bowl, toss the nuts with the egg white to coat in a thin, even layer. Add the salt, brown sugar, and cumin. Stir to combine.

Spread the nuts on the prepared baking sheet. Bake for 30 minutes, stirring every 10 minutes.

Let cool and store in an airtight container for up to 6 months.

Comté & Buckwheat Pesto

This pesto is a great way to use up wilting greens or leftover cheese rinds. It's endlessly adaptable with different herbs, lettuces, cheeses, and nuts.

MAKES ABOUT 1 ¼ CUPS (300 G)
PREP TIME: 20 MINUTES
BAKE TIME: 20 TO 30 MINUTES

¼ CUP (50 G) BUCKWHEAT
1 BUNCH PARSLEY, ABOUT 3 ½ OZ (100 G)
3 ½ OZ (100 G) ARUGULA OR MIXED GREENS
2 GARLIC CLOVES, PEELED
3 ½ OZ (100 G) COMTÉ CHEESE WITH RIND, CHOPPED
¾ CUP (180 ML) OLIVE OIL
2 TSP BLACK PEPPERCORNS
1 TSP FLEUR DE SEL
2 ICE CUBES

Preheat the oven to 320°F (160°C).

Spread the buckwheat on a baking sheet and toast for 20 to 30 minutes until golden blond.

In a blender or food processor, combine the parsley (including stems), arugula, garlic, cheese, olive oil, peppercorns, fleur de sel, and cooled buckwheat. Blend, adding the ice cubes one at a time to emulsify.

Enjoy immediately or refrigerate for up to 1 month.

Pistachio & Pumpkin Seed Spread

Think of this as a riff on Nutella, but with pistachios, pumpkin seeds, and white chocolate.

MAKES TWO 10-OZ (300-ML) JARS
PREP TIME: 15 MINUTES
BAKE TIME: 25 MINUTES

7 OZ (200 G) UNSALTED PISTACHIOS, SHELLED
7 OZ (200 G) PUMPKIN SEEDS
½ CUP (120 G) SUGAR
3 OZ (90 G) WHITE CHOCOLATE, CHOPPED
1 PINCH FLEUR DE SEL
1 ½ TBSP NEUTRAL OIL

Preheat the oven to 320°F (160°C). Line a baking sheet with parchment paper.

Spread the pistachios and pumpkin seeds on the prepared baking sheet and toast for 20 minutes.

In a saucepan, gently boil 2 tbsp of water and the sugar to a light caramel, about 350°F (175°C). Pour the caramel over the toasted nuts and let cool.

Once cool, transfer the nuts to a food processor and blend until smooth. Add the white chocolate (unmelted), fleur de sel, and oil. The chocolate will melt from the heat generated by blending.

Transfer to the jars. Store in a cool, dark place for up to 1 year.

Homemade Mustard

I love mustard. My friend Tristan and I tested countless batches for months until we realized the key was using yellow mustard seeds, not black. Use this mustard as-is for vinaigrettes or as a condiment for meats. If you prefer a smoother texture, just pop it in the blender.

MAKES ONE 10-OZ (300-ML) JAR
PREP TIME: 5 MINUTES
FERMENTATION: OVERNIGHT

3 ½ OZ (100 G) YELLOW MUSTARD SEEDS
¾ CUP (180 ML) WHITE VINEGAR
1 TBSP HONEY
10 BLACK PEPPERCORNS

In a clean jar, combine the mustard seeds, vinegar, honey, and peppercorns. Seal and let ferment at room temperature overnight.

The next day, open the jar briefly to release any gas.

Store in the refrigerator for up to 6 months.

Sliced Almond Florentines

These lacey and crispy cookies are big on flavor and easy to make. For this recipe, you'll need at least twenty 3-inch (8-cm) tartlet molds.

MAKES 20 TARTLETS
PREP TIME: 15 MINUTES
BAKE TIME: 25 MINUTES

1 LB (450 G) VANILLA SWEET PASTRY DOUGH (PAGE 45)
3 OZ (90 G) BUTTER
3 ¼ OZ (92 G) SUGAR
¼ CUP (60 ML) HEAVY CREAM
2 ½ OZ (75 G) MOUNTAIN OR CHESTNUT HONEY
7 ¾ OZ (220 G) SLICED ALMONDS

Preheat the oven to 320°F (160°C). Grease the tartlet molds.

On a floured surface, roll the pastry to ⅛ inch (3 mm) thick. Prick with a fork and cut out 3-inch (8-cm) rounds. Press into 3-inch (8-cm) tartlet molds. Bake for 15 minutes until lightly golden.

Meanwhile, in a saucepan, combine the butter, sugar, cream, and honey. Bring to a boil and cook until the mixture reaches 245°F (120°C). Remove from the heat and stir in the almonds.

Spoon about ¾ oz (20 g) of the mixture into each tartlet. Increase the oven temperature to 340°F (170°C), then return the tartlets to the oven for 10 minutes. Remove from the oven and let cool before serving.

Store in an airtight container at room temperature for up to 2 weeks.

Cocoa Florentines

If you're using raw buckwheat, it should first be lightly toasted for 1 hour. (Kasha is already toasted buckwheat.) For this recipe, you'll need at least twenty 3-inch (8-cm) tartlet molds.

MAKES 20 TARTLETS
PREP TIME: 15 MINUTES
BAKE TIME: 25 MINUTES

1 LB (450 G) COCOA SWEET PASTRY DOUGH (PAGE 34)
3 OZ (90 G) BUTTER
3 ¼ OZ (92 G) SUGAR
¼ CUP (60 ML) HEAVY CREAM
2 ½ OZ (75 G) MOUNTAIN OR CHESTNUT HONEY
3 ¾ OZ (110 G) COCOA NIBS
3 ¾ OZ (110 G) TOASTED BUCKWHEAT OR KASHA
1 TBSP UNSWEETENED COCOA POWDER

Preheat the oven to 320°F (160°C).

Roll the cocoa pastry to ⅛ inch (3 mm) thick. Prick with a fork and cut out 3-inch (8 cm) rounds. Press into 3-inch (8-cm) tartlet molds. Bake for 15 minutes.

Meanwhile, combine the butter, sugar, cream, and honey in a medium saucepan. Bring to a boil and heat to 245°F (120°C). Remove from the heat and add the cocoa nibs, toasted buckwheat or kasha, and cocoa powder.

Spoon about ¾ oz (20 g) of the mixture into each tartlet. Increase the oven temperature to 340°F (170°C), then return the tartlets to the oven for 10 minutes. Remove from the oven and let cool before serving.

Store in an airtight container at room temperature for up to 2 weeks.

Buckwheat-Almond Praliné

Praline vs. praliné: The two sweets are similar, but the former is a soft candy with nuts where the latter is a paste made from grinding nuts with sugar. For this recipe, the addition of oil is essential, as buckwheat is low in fat, and fat is key to achieving a silky texture.

MAKES TWO 13-OZ (380-ML) JARS
PREP TIME: 15 MINUTES
COOK TIME: 25 MINUTES

2 ½ CUPS (340 G) RAW ALMONDS
1 ½ CUPS (226 G) TOASTED BUCKWHEAT OR KASHA*
¾ CUP (170 G) SUGAR
SEEDS FROM 1 VANILLA BEAN, SCRAPED
¼ CUP (60 ML) NEUTRAL OIL

Preheat the oven to 320°F (160°C). Line a baking sheet with parchment paper.

Spread the almonds and toasted buckwheat or kasha on the prepared baking sheet. Roast in the oven for 20 minutes.

In a saucepan, bring ¼ cup (60 ml) of water and the sugar to a gentle boil and cook until a light amber caramel forms, about 350°F (175°C). Pour over the toasted nuts and let cool.

Transfer the caramelized mixture to a food processor (not a blender). Add the vanilla seeds and blend until the mixture is sandy. Slowly add the oil and continue blending until smooth and spreadable.

Store in sterilized jars at room temperature for up to 1 year.

** If using raw buckwheat, toast for 1 hour before beginning the recipe.*

Hazelnut, Almond & Dark Chocolate Spread

MAKES TWO 10-OZ (300-ML) JARS
PREP TIME: 15 MINUTES
COOK TIME: 25 MINUTES

1 ⅓ CUPS (200 G) HAZELNUTS
1 ⅓ CUPS (200 G) RAW ALMONDS
½ CUP (120 G) SUGAR
3 OZ (90 G) DARK CHOCOLATE, CHOPPED
PINCH OF FLEUR DE SEL
1 ½ TBSP NEUTRAL OIL

Preheat the oven to 320°F (160°C). Line a baking sheet with parchment paper.

Spread the hazelnuts and almonds on the prepared baking sheet. Toast in the oven for 20 minutes.

In a saucepan, bring 2 tbsp of water and the sugar to a gentle boil and cook until a light amber caramel forms, about 350°F (175°C). Pour over the toasted nuts and let cool.

Transfer everything to a food processor and blend until smooth. Add the chopped (not melted) chocolate, fleur de sel, and oil. The heat from the processor will melt the chocolate as it mixes.

Transfer to sterilized jars and store in a cool, dark place for up to 1 year.

Christophe Adam's Caramel Nut Tart

My pastry chef friend Christophe Adam is never far from my thoughts. I always consult him when I have a big decision to make–such as making this tart. This is a weighty recipe, but it's well worth the effort.

SERVES 8
PREP TIME: 1 HOUR
CHILL TIME: 4 HOURS
BAKE TIME: 30 MINUTES

HAZELNUT SWEET TART DOUGH

¾ CUP (85 G) SIFTED POWDERED SUGAR
3 TBSP ALMOND FLOUR
1 TBSP HAZELNUT FLOUR
½ TSP SALT
1 ½ TBSP VANILLA SUGAR
9 TBSP BUTTER, SOFTENED
1 EGG
1 ½ CUPS (195 G) ALL-PURPOSE FLOUR

CARAMEL CREAM

1 ¼ TSP GELATIN
1 VANILLA BEAN, SPLIT AND SCRAPED
1 ½ CUPS (360 ML) HEAVY CREAM, WARMED
1 CUP (200 G) GRANULATED SUGAR
1 ½ TBSP GLUCOSE SYRUP
6 EGG YOLKS, BEATEN

CARAMEL GLAZE

½ CUP (100 G) GRANULATED SUGAR
¾ CUP (180 ML) NEUTRAL GLAZE

CARAMELIZED HAZELNUTS

⅔ CUP (100 G) HAZELNUTS
⅓ CUP (50 G) POWDERED SUGAR

CARAMELIZED PEANUTS

⅓ CUP (50 G) PEANUTS
2 TBSP POWDERED SUGAR

CARAMELIZED COCOA NIBS

⅓ CUP (50 G) COCOA NIBS
2 TBSP POWDERED SUGAR

ASSEMBLY

⅓ CUP (50 G) TOASTED ALMONDS, CHOPPED

Hazelnut Sweet Tart Dough

In a stand mixer fitted with the paddle attachment, combine the sifted powdered sugar, almond and hazelnut flours, salt, and vanilla sugar with the softened butter. Cream until smooth. Add the egg and mix again.

Add the all-purpose flour and mix by hand just until the dough comes together. Avoid overworking to prevent gluten development.

Wrap the dough in plastic wrap and refrigerate for at least 2 hours. Grease a 9-inch (22-cm) tart pan.

Roll the dough out to ⅛ inch (3 mm) thick and transfer it to the prepared tart pan. Prick the base with a fork, and chill for at least 1 hour.

Preheat the oven to 320°F (160°C). Bake for 20 minutes or until evenly golden.

Caramel Cream

In a small bowl, soak the gelatin in 1 tbsp of cold water for at least 30 minutes.

In a separate bowl, infuse the vanilla bean and seeds in the warm cream.

In a small saucepan, make a dark caramel by combining the sugar, ¼ cup (60 ml) water, and glucose syrup. Heat over medium high, occasionally swirling the pan but not stirring until the mixture reaches 365°F (185° C) and turns a dark copper color. Remove the vanilla bean and gradually pour in the warm cream to stop the cooking. Remove from the heat.

In a separate bowl, whisk a portion of the caramel cream into the egg yolks to temper them, then return everything to the saucepan. Cook over medium heat, stirring constantly, until it reaches 185°F (85°C).

Remove from the heat and stir in the gelatin. Blend with an immersion blender.

Caramel Glaze

Place the sugar in a small saucepan. Cook over low-medium heat and allow to caramelize. Do not stir. Once golden in color, carefully deglaze with ⅓ cup (80 ml) water and remove from the heat. Stir in the neutral glaze.

Caramelized Hazelnuts, Peanuts, and Cocoa Nibs

In a saucepan, combine the hazelnuts and powdered sugar. Cook over medium heat, stirring constantly, until the nuts are coated in a sandy sugar layer and begin to caramelize. Remove from the heat. Repeat these instructions with the peanuts and then the cocoa nibs.

Assembly

Pour the caramel cream into the tart shell, leaving a ⅛-inch (3-mm) gap at the top. Refrigerate for at least 1 hour.

Once set, spread the caramel glaze over the top using an offset spatula. Sprinkle with the caramelized nuts and cocoa nibs and finish with the toasted almonds.

5

DAIRY & PLANT-BASED ALTERNATIVES

Dairy is part of the very DNA of pastry. So, my philosophy is that if I make the bread and I make the jam, I absolutely must make the butter too—it's the only way to get the perfect slice of toast. Of course, If you choose to only make the bread, the jam, or the butter, that's okay too. This chapter explores flavorful plant-based milks and corresponding recipes as well.

Homemade Buckwheat Butter

MAKES ABOUT 7.5 OZ (215 G)
PREP TIME: 20 MINUTES
COOK TIME: 20 MINUTES

1 CUP (240 ML) HEAVY CREAM
1 CUP (250 G) GOOD QUALITY CRÈME FRAÎCHE
⅓ CUP (50 G) TOASTED BUCKWHEAT OR KASHA*
¾ TSP MALDON SALT

Using a stand mixer with a whisk attachment, whip the creams until the mixture separates into butter and buttermilk. First it will become whipped cream, then it will split. Drain the butter in a fine-mesh sieve and rinse it thoroughly under very cold water to remove all the buttermilk, which can cause rancidity. Repeat until the water runs clear, then drain well.

Meanwhile, preheat the oven to 350°F (175°C). Line a baking sheet with parchment paper.

Spread the toasted buckwheat on the prepared baking sheet and refresh the flavor by toasting for 20 minutes. Let cool, then crush the buckwheat between two pieces of parchment paper with the bottom of a saucepan.

In the stand mixer with the paddle attachment, combine the homemade butter and the Maldon salt and mix. Fold in the crushed buckwheat using a spatula.

Store the butter in an airtight container in the fridge for up to 10 days.

** If using raw buckwheat, toast for 1 hour before beginning the recipe. This deepens the flavor. (Kasha is already toasted.)*

Raspberry-Vanilla Compound Butter

Try this delicious butter on your morning toast or slather on a homemade scone.

MAKES ABOUT 1 CUP (260 G)
PREP TIME: 20 MINUTES

8 RASPBERRIES
1 ¼ CUPS (300 ML) HEAVY CREAM
1 ¼ CUPS (300 G) GOOD QUALITY CRÈME FRAÎCHE
SEEDS OF 1 VANILLA BEAN, SCRAPED

Place the raspberries in the freezer. The idea is to just barely freeze them to preserve their texture.

In the bowl of a stand mixer with the whisk attachment, beat the creams until butter forms. The mixture will first turn into whipped cream, then separate into butter and buttermilk. It's important to rinse the butter several times under very cold water using a fine-mesh strainer to remove all the buttermilk, as this is what causes butter to go rancid. Repeat until the water runs clear, then drain thoroughly.

In the stand mixer with a paddle attachment, mix the butter with the vanilla seeds.

Remove the raspberries from the freezer and crush them using a rolling pin or the bottom of a saucepan to separate the drupelets. Add the crushed frozen raspberries to the mixer and briefly mix again.

Store in an airtight container in the fridge for up to 10 days.

Pumpkin Seed Milk

Homemade plant milks are delicate and have a short shelf life. For longer storage, boil the sealed bottle in a pot of water for 1 hour, then refrigerate. This extends the unopened shelf life to about 15 days. You can lightly sweeten the pumpkin seed milk by adding sugar. You can also flavor it with vanilla or spices if desired.

MAKES ONE 1-QUART (1-L) JAR
PREP TIME: 20 MINUTES
COOK TIME: 20 MINUTES
SOAKING: OVERNIGHT

7 OZ (200 G) RAW PUMPKIN SEEDS
¼ CUP (50 G) SUGAR (OPTIONAL)

Preheat the oven to 320°F (160°C). Line a baking sheet with parchment paper.

Spread the pumpkin seeds on the prepared baking sheet and toast for 20 minutes. Immediately transfer the seeds to a large bowl of water and soak overnight.

The next day, drain and discard the soaking water. Transfer the seeds to a blender or food processor. Begin blending, gradually adding 1 quart (1 L) water to form a smooth paste. You can sweeten the milk by adding the sugar. Blend for about 3 minutes.

Strain the milk through a clean, fine-weave cloth to extract the solids and collect only the liquid.

Sterilize a glass bottle or quart (liter) jar by pouring in boiling water and boiling the cap separately. Dump out the water once it cools.

Pour the milk into the sterilized bottle and refrigerate for 3 to 4 days.

Orange Blossom Almond Milk

As mentioned in the previous recipe, homemade plant milks are delicate and have a short shelf life. For longer storage, boil the sealed bottle in a pot of water for 1 hour, then refrigerate. This extends the unopened shelf life to about 15 days.

MAKES ONE 1-QUART (1-L) JAR
PREP TIME: 15 MINUTES
SOAKING: OVERNIGHT

1 ⅓ CUPS (200 G) BLANCHED ALMONDS
1 ¼ TSP ORANGE BLOSSOM WATER
SEEDS OF 1 VANILLA BEAN, SCRAPED
¼ CUP (50 G) GRANULATED SUGAR (OPTIONAL)

Place the almonds in a bowl of water and soak overnight.

The next day, drain and rinse the almonds, discarding the soaking water. Transfer the almonds to a blender or food processor. Begin blending, gradually adding 1 quart (1 L) of water to create a smooth paste. Blend for 3 minutes.

Strain the mixture through a clean, fine-weave cloth to remove the solids and collect only the milk. Stir in the orange blossom water and vanilla seeds. You can sweeten the milk by adding the sugar.

Sterilize a glass bottle or quart (liter) jar by pouring in boiling water and boiling the cap separately. Dump out the water once it cools.

Pour the milk into the sterilized bottle or jar and refrigerate for 3 to 4 days.

Almond Milk Porridge

Everyone in the house teases me for always having porridge on the menu, even though I'm the only one who eats it. Here's my go-to recipe for all the other porridge lovers out there. For what to do with your apple scraps, see Apple-Ginger Drink (page 135).

SERVES 2
PREP TIME: 5 MINUTES
COOK TIME: 2 MINUTES

2 CUPS (480 ML) ORANGE BLOSSOM ALMOND MILK (PAGE 171)
1 CUP (100 G) ROLLED OATS
¼ CUP (60 ML) WILDFLOWER HONEY
1 BOSKOOP APPLE OR OTHER TART VARIETY, PEELED, CORED, AND CUT INTO MATCHSTICKS
1 CONFERENCE PEAR, PEELED, CORED, AND CUT INTO MATCHSTICKS
JUICE FROM ½ LEMON

In a medium saucepan, bring the almond milk and oats to a boil. Reduce the heat and cook for 2 minutes, stirring constantly. Remove from the heat and stir in the honey.

Toss the apple and pear with the lemon juice. Serve the fruit on top of or on the side of the porridge.

Oven-Baked Rice Pudding

This rice pudding is best enjoyed warm after resting. If preparing ahead, refrigerate and loosen by stirring in 1 cup (240 ml) of whipped cream before serving.

SERVES 6
PREP TIME: 15 MINUTES
COOK TIME: 35 MINUTES
RESTING TIME: 1 HOUR

4 CUPS (1 L) WHOLE MILK
2 CUPS (480 ML) HEAVY CREAM, DIVIDED
2 VANILLA BEANS, SPLIT AND SCRAPED
1 ¼ CUPS (250 G) SHORT-GRAIN RICE
3 ½ OZ (100 G) WHITE CHOCOLATE, CHOPPED

Preheat the oven to 320°F (160°C).

In a large saucepan, bring the milk and half the cream to a boil with the vanilla pods and seeds. Cover with a lid and remove from the heat.

Meanwhile, place the rice in a large saucepan and add 2 ½ cups (600 ml) of water. Bring to a boil to blanch the rice—this breaks the outer layer for better absorption.

Once boiling, remove from the heat, drain the rice, and transfer to an oven-safe baking dish. Pour the hot milk mixture over it, cover tightly with foil, and bake for 30 minutes.

Remove from the oven, stir in the remaining cream and the white chocolate. Remove the vanilla pods and let dessert rest for 1 hour so the rice can finish absorbing the liquid.

Creamy Scrambled Eggs

I love eggs, especially when they're finished with cream or fresh goat cheese.

SERVES 2
PREP TIME: 10 MINUTES
COOK TIME: 5 MINUTES

4 EXTRA-FRESH EGGS
SALT AND PEPPER
FRESH NUTMEG
¼ CUP (50 G) CRÈME FRAÎCHE
3 ½ OZ (100 G) FRESH GOAT CHEESE, CRUMBLED
1 BUNCH CHIVES, FINELY CHOPPED

Bring a medium saucepan of water to a boil.

In a medium glass or metal mixing bowl (wider than the saucepan so it can be the top of a double boiler), whisk the eggs with salt, pepper, and freshly grated nutmeg.

Place the bowl over the saucepan to cook the eggs gently, stirring slowly with a whisk. Once the eggs reach a creamy texture, remove from the heat and stir in the crème fraîche to stop the cooking.

Spoon into serving bowls. Top with crumbled goat cheese and chives.

Savory Homemade Yogurt

I eat a lot of yogurt. Sweet or savory, it's one of my favorite protein staples.

MAKES ABOUT 3 CUPS (730 G)
PREP TIME: 20 MINUTES
COOK TIME: 5 HOURS
CHILL TIME: OVERNIGHT

2 CUPS (480 ML) WHOLE MILK
½ CUP (70 G) POWDERED MILK
⅔ CUP (160 ML) HEAVY CREAM
1 PACKET BULGARIAN YOGURT STARTER
SALT
OLIVE OIL
ZA'ATAR

Sterilize a heatproof quart (liter) jar.

In a medium saucepan, heat the milk, powdered milk, and cream to 195°F (90°C). Cool the mixture down to 111°F (44°C), then whisk in the yogurt starter.

Pour into the quart jar, seal, and incubate in a 105°F (40°C) oven for 5 hours.

Refrigerate overnight.

When ready to serve, stir the yogurt in a bowl until smooth. Season with a pinch of salt, a drizzle of olive oil, and a sprinkle of za'atar. Serve with fresh herbs and salad greens.

Christophe Adam's Yogurt Cake with Salted Caramel

This cake perfectly balances tangy with sweet.

SERVES 8
PREP TIME: 20 MINUTES
BAKE TIME: 20 MINUTES

YOGURT CAKE

½ CUP (125 G) PLAIN YOGURT OR SAVORY HOMEMADE YOGURT (PAGE 179)
1 ¼ CUPS (250 G) SUGAR
2 CUPS (250 G) FLOUR
3 EGGS
1 ½ TSP BAKING POWDER
⅓ CUP (80 ML) VEGETABLE OIL

SALTED BUTTER CARAMEL

½ CUP (100 G) SUGAR
½ CUP (120 ML) HEAVY CREAM
2 TBSP SALTED BUTTER

To make the yogurt cake, preheat the oven to 350°F (175°C). Butter and flour a round 9-inch (22-cm) cake pan.

In a mixing bowl, whisk together the yogurt and sugar. Add the flour, eggs, and baking powder. Finish by stirring in the oil with a wooden spoon or spatula. The batter should be smooth and well combined.

Pour into the prepared cake pan and bake for 15 to 20 minutes, until golden and a knife inserted in the center comes out clean. Remove from the oven and let cool.

To make the salted butter caramel, heat the sugar in a medium saucepan over medium heat without stirring. You can swirl the pan gently to help the sugar melt evenly. Once it turns into a smooth golden syrup, remove from the heat.

In a separate saucepan, bring the cream to a simmer. Off the heat, carefully pour the hot cream into the caramel. (Never use cold cream, or the caramel will seize. Stir in the butter and return to the heat, stirring with a spatula until smooth.

Remove the cake from the pan and place on a serving plate. Slowly pour the hot caramel over the top, spreading it evenly. Let cool before slicing.

6

BREAD

In every culture, bread appears in one form or another. It's more than just food; each loaf embodies real values of sharing and respect. That is why I never throw out leftovers.

Yesterday and Tomorrow's Bread

My vision of bread is shaped by my background in pastry. I approach bread like I would a dessert, and I enjoy creating a variety of types. I also love sourcing flours—there's an incredible diversity of flavor in wheat varieties. It's no coincidence that bread is at the heart of the diet in many cultures. Bread is nourishing, wholesome, and it feeds life.

That is why I hold bread in such high regard. I wanted to extend its life beyond the usual routes of croutons or rusks (which are already great options). That's how "yesterday and tomorrow's bread" was born—it's a continuation of my mission to avoid waste.

On a trip to Austria with my friend, Chef Pierre Reboul, I discovered the old practice of reusing bread in bread. This clever technique had been banned in France for sanitary reasons, but we found a way to adapt and safely reintroduce it.

With help from Pierre in our lab, we developed a recipe we truly love. First, we dry the bread thoroughly and grind it. Then we turn it into a kind of bread cream, which becomes the base for a new dough that ferments and proofs over three days. We now reuse about 30 percent of our unsold bread, getting every last bit of value from it.

It's a virtuous circle. In fact, we can even make "yesterday and tomorrow's bread" using…yesterday and tomorrow's bread.

300
400

Homemade Croutons

Croutons are a perfect way to use up leftover bread. Serve them with salads, soups, sautéed vegetables, or seasonal mushrooms. They also freeze well for future use.

MAKES ABOUT 3 CUPS (400 G)
PREP TIME: 10 MINUTES
RESTING TIME: 10 MINUTES
COOK TIME: 5 MINUTES

2 GARLIC CLOVES
⅔ CUP (160 ML) OLIVE OIL
10 BLACK PEPPERCORNS
PINCH FINE SALT
3 SPRIGS FRESH THYME, LEAVES ONLY
3 CUPS (400 G) STALE BREAD, CUT INTO ¾-INCH (2-CM) CUBES

In a blender, combine the garlic, olive oil, peppercorns, salt, and thyme leaves. Blend until smooth.

Pour the flavored oil over the bread cubes and let them soak for 10 minutes.

Heat a large skillet and toast the croutons over high heat until golden.

Homemade Melba Toast

Serve cracker-like melba toast with a variety of spreads and dips, terrines, charcuterie platters, and even soup. You can either specifically make melbas (see below) or think of them as a way to lessen waste: If you know you're not going to finish a loaf of bread, slice it thinly and bake it until crisp.

FOR 1 LOAF OF SANDWICH BREAD (ABOUT 15 OZ)
PREP TIME: 40 MINUTES
RESTING TIME: 30 MINUTES
CHILL TIME: OVERNIGHT
BAKE TIME: 1 HOUR 5 MINUTES

3 TBSP BUTTER, DICED
2 CUPS (250 G) ALL-PURPOSE FLOUR, PLUS MORE FOR SHAPING
¾ CUP (195 G) WATER
2 TSP GRANULATED SUGAR
1 EGG
2 TSP FRESH YEAST
1 TSP SALT
2 TSP POWDERED MILK OR 1 ½ TBSP WHOLE MILK
NEUTRAL OIL FOR THE PAN

The day before, prepare the sandwich bread: Soften the butter in the microwave at low intervals until creamy. In the bowl of a stand mixer set with a dough hook, combine all other ingredients, ensuring the salt doesn't come into direct contact with the yeast.

Add the softened butter and knead with the dough hook for 7 minutes on low speed, then 12 minutes on high. Shape into a ball and let rest for 20 minutes on a floured surface.

Punch down the dough and shape into an oval (also called a bâtard).

Place in a greased loaf pan. Let rise for 30 minutes at room temperature, covered with a damp cloth.

Preheat the oven to 400°F (200°C). Place a heavy tray on top and bake for 45 minutes. Remove tray and let cool, then refrigerate overnight.

The next day, slice bread into ½-inch (1 cm) pieces. Arrange on a parchment-lined baking sheet. Preheat oven to 350°F (180°C) and bake for 20 minutes.

Store in a dry place for up to one month.

Cumin & Hazelnut Breadsticks

MAKES ABOUT 10
PREP TIME: 20 MINUTES
RESTING TIME: 1 HOUR
BAKE TIME: 12 MINUTES

2 TSP FRESH YEAST OR ACTIVE DRY YEAST
2 ¾ CUPS (330 G) BREAD FLOUR
1 ½ TBSP SUGAR
1 TSP SALT
1 ¼ CUPS (300 ML) OLIVE OIL, PLUS MORE FOR BRUSHING
¼ CUP (30 G) HAZELNUTS, CHOPPED
PINCH CUMIN SEEDS
PINCH FLEUR DE SEL

Line a baking sheet with parchment paper.

If using fresh yeast, combine the yeast, flour, sugar, salt, 1 ¼ cups (300 ml) water, and olive oil in the bowl of a stand mixer fitted with the dough hook. Knead on low speed for 7 minutes until smooth and slightly elastic.

If using dry yeast, combine the yeast with 1 ¼ cups (300 ml) water in the bowl of a stand mixer fitted with the dough hook and let stand for about 5 minutes. Then add the flour, sugar, salt, and olive oil. Knead on low speed for 7 minutes until smooth and slightly elastic.

Transfer the dough (made with either kind of yeast) to the prepared baking sheet brushed with a little olive oil. Let rest for 1 hour at room temperature under a damp cloth.

Preheat the oven to 400°F (200°C).

Cut the dough into ten ¾-inch (2-cm) squares about 1 ½ oz (50 g) each, then roll each piece into a thin rope about the length of your baking sheet, roughly ½ inch (1 cm) thick.

Brush the breadsticks with olive oil and sprinkle with chopped hazelnuts, cumin seeds, and fleur de sel.

Bake for 12 minutes. Enjoy immediately or store in a cool, dry place out of direct sunlight.

Focaccia

SERVES 4 TO 5
PREP TIME: 15 MINUTES
RESTING TIME: 1 HOUR 30 MINUTES
BAKE TIME: 10 TO 12 MINUTES

2 CUPS (250 G) FLOUR
2 TSP FRESH YEAST OR ACTIVE DRY YEAST
PINCH DRIED OREGANO
PINCH SALT
¼ CUP (60 ML) OLIVE OIL, DIVIDED
10 CHERRY TOMATOES, HALVED
1 SPRIG THYME, LEAVES ONLY
FLEUR DE SEL

If using fresh yeast, in the bowl of a stand mixer fitted with a dough hook, combine the flour, yeast, 1 cup (240 ml) water, oregano, and salt. Knead on medium speed for 2 to 3 minutes, then on high speed for 7 to 8 minutes.

If using dry yeast, in the bowl of a stand mixer fitted with a dough hook, combine 1 cup (240 ml) water with the yeast and let stand for 5 minutes. Then add the flour, oregano, and salt. Knead on medium speed for 2 to 3 minutes, then on high speed for 7 to 8 minutes.

Cover the dough (made with either kind of yeast) with a damp cloth and let rest at room temperature for 30 minutes.

Place an 8-inch (20-cm) round ring mold on a baking sheet. Flatten your dough, add to the ring mold, and brush with the olive oil. Let rise for 1 hour at room temperature or in a turned-off oven.

Preheat the oven to 465°F (240°C).

Poke dimples in the dough with your fingers and brush again with olive oil. Top with the cherry tomatoes and sprinkle with the thyme leaves.

Bake for 10 to 12 minutes.

Out of the oven, brush again with olive oil and sprinkle with fleur de sel.

Vegetarian Croque-Monsieur

MAKES 6 SANDWICHES
PREP TIME: 15 MINUTES
COOK TIME: 6 MINUTES

7 TBSP BUTTER
2 CUPS (500 G) MASCARPONE CHEESE
2 CUPS (250 G) GRATED EMMENTAL CHEESE
1 ZUCCHINI
12 SLICES SANDWICH BREAD
½ CUP (120 G) COMTÉ & BUCKWHEAT PESTO (PAGE 142)
2 SPRIGS BASIL, LEAVES ONLY

In a saucepan, gently melt the butter, then let it sit so the milk solids separate and clarify.

In a large bowl, soften the mascarpone by stirring with a spatula, then fold in the grated Emmental.

Slice the zucchini into thin ribbons using a mandoline, then cut to fit the bread slices.

Brush one side of each bread slice with clarified butter. Lay six slices butter-side down on a parchment-lined surface. Spread about ¼ cup (60 g) of the cheese mixture onto the other side of the slices. Then layer the zucchini, pesto, and basil leaves on top of the cheese mixture.

Spread the remaining cheese mixture on the remaining six slices and close the sandwiches.

Heat a skillet (no oil needed) and brown the sandwiches for 3 minutes on each side. Slice each sandwich in half and serve immediately.

Chef Coly's Chicken Liver Terrine

Chef Didier Coly and I have known each other for more than twenty years. He's had a huge impact on my professional life and has an incredible depth of product knowledge. I'll concede that this is an odd recipe to add to a bread section, but my reasoning is that this terrine should only be served with thin slices of excellent homemade bread or homemade melba toast.

MAKES ABOUT 3 LB (1 ⅓ KG)
PREP TIME: 20 MINUTES
RESTING TIME: OVERNIGHT
COOK TIME: 2 HOURS 30 MINUTES

1 LB (450 G) GROUND CHICKEN LIVERS
2 LB (900 G) GROUND PORK JOWLS*
3 GARLIC CLOVES, FINELY CHOPPED
1 ONION, FINELY CHOPPED
1 BUNCH FRESH PARSLEY, FINELY CHOPPED
1 TBSP BLACK PEPPERCORNS, CRUSHED
1 SPRIG THYME, LEAVES ONLY
1 TBSP SALT
2 TSP QUATRE ÉPICES
1 BAY LEAF
1 TBSP SUGAR
2 TBSP COGNAC
½ CUP (120 ML) HEAVY CREAM
SANDWICH BREAD OR HOMEMADE MELBA TOAST (PAGE 196) FOR SERVING

In a large bowl, combine the ground meats with the chopped garlic, onion, and parsley.

Add the peppercorns, thyme leaves, salt, quatre épices, bay leaf, sugar, Cognac, and heavy cream. Mix thoroughly by hand, cover with plastic wrap, and let rest overnight in the refrigerator.

The next day preheat the oven to 250°F (120°C).

Remove the bay leaf and transfer the mixture to a ceramic or stoneware terrine. Press down firmly to eliminate air pockets.

Bake for 2 ½ hours. Let cool completely, then refrigerate. Keeps for up to 3 weeks. Eat sliced with toasted bread or spread on crackers or melba toast.

* *Ask your butcher to grind the chicken livers and pork jowls.*

APPENDICES

Recipes A to Z

Index by Ingredients

Acknowledgments

Thank you to Éditions de La Martinière, Laure Aline, and Agathe Masson, for trusting me not once, not twice, but three times (I know, that one's too easy).

To Guillaume Czerw—this one's even better than the first two! He really should consider a career in photography.

To Tristan Rolland for his boundless creative energy.

To Clément Rivalin, the man behind the scenes. With him, everything runs like clockwork. Nothing ever slips by.

To Didier Coly for his unwavering support and legendary positivity.

To Pierre Reboul, for our endless deep dives and life debriefs.

To Christophe Adam, my favorite challenger (you made that, now I want to make this).

To Pascal Lafaye for the morning texts that always bring a smile.

To Vincent Lappartient for his eagle eye and natural style.

To Christophe Felder, never far away. He really should write books—it suits him.

Thank you Margot, my daughter, always the crème de la crème.

Thank you Camille, for your talent for spotting the tiniest details and always saying just the right three words.

Thank you to my dear mom for her beautifully kept garden.

Thank you Océane and Emmanuel, two amazing gardeners.

They've never let me down. They're always there.

The Seasonal Pantry was first published in
the United States by Tra Publishing in 2026.

U.S. Edition

Publisher and Creative Director
Ilona Oppenheim

Art & Design Director
Jefferson Quintana

Editorial Director
Lisa McGuinness

Publishing Director
Jessica Faroy

Senior Designer
Morgane Leoni

Illustrator
Maisy Summer

Tra Eats Editor
Amanda M. Faison

The Seasonal Pantry was first published in France under the title:
Garde-manger de Benoît Castel (Le). 75 recettes à conserver pour bien manger plus tard

Printed and bound in China by Artron Art Co., Ltd.

This product is made of FSC®-certified and other controlled material.

Tra Publishing is committed to sustainability in its materials and practices.

ISBN: 978-1-962098-37-3

Tra Publishing
245 NE 37th Street
Miami, FL 33137
trapublishing.com

tra.publishing

12345678910